i

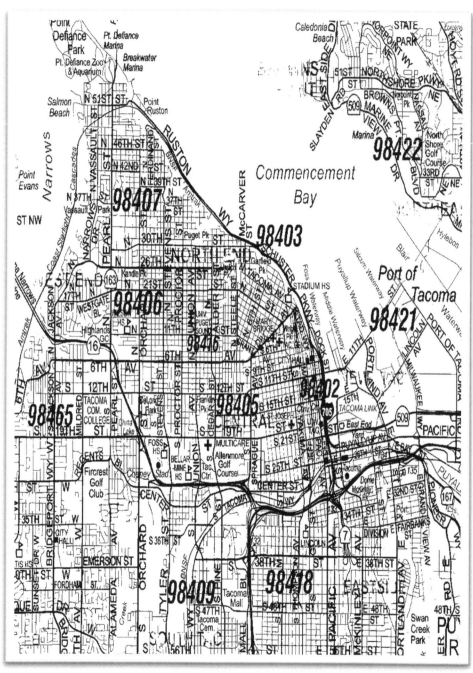

Tacoma, Washington

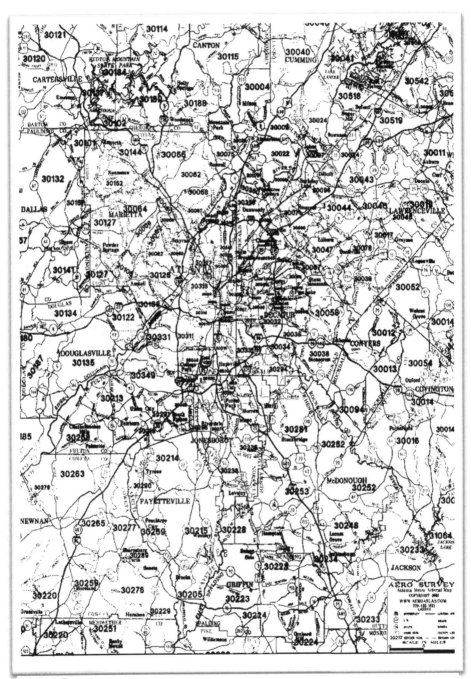

Atlanta, Georgia

Praise for
"Principals Don't Walk on Water: They Walk Through It"

"This book provides one of the most realistic looks at the challenge of being an educational activist. Educators choose their profession to make a positive impact on their students and communities, but face obstacles that the common citizen would never imagine. This book is an important testimonial for all the men and women who lead schools on a daily basis, who don't just deserve our admiration, but our support."

> *-Dr. Anthony Muhammad,*
> *Author & Educational Consultant*

"Andre Benito Mountain is a modern-day Renaissance Man! Like me, he is a teacher and leader who likes to teach students to play chess and about Hip-Hop culture. Andre has inspired thousands of educators to embrace culture and arts implementation with fidelity and excellence! He is making an impact on students and teachers around the nation. In his new book, Principals don't Walk on Water, he has written the blueprint for school leaders who want to become resilient and find their purpose. It is a must read for every educator!"

> *-Salome Thomas-EL, Ed.D,*
> *Award-winning Principal & Author*

"People outside of education don't have a clue what it takes to mold young minds into the leaders of tomorrow. For that matter, many of those who guide and manage the schools themselves are too frequently out of touch. That's why the writings of Andre Benito Mountain are so important - and timely. Andre peels back the veil that obscures an objective examination not only of the classroom, but of administration and policy development. Based on years of personal experience, Andre leaves us better informed parents and citizens and inspires us to demand greater accountability."

-Bob Young, Former Mayor of Augusta, Georgia

"Mr. Mountain is a thought provoking and inspirational change agent who challenges the status quo and redefines "excellence". His work as an author and educational leader represents innovation and most importantly, the application of innovation in the evolving landscape of public education. The principles, concepts, ideas and strategies that Mr. Mountain describes in his works are invaluable to the field of education. His intellect is highlighted through his ability to share how his life experiences, professional and personal, have shaped his personal ideology on the purpose of education, education reform and the future of this great profession."

-Dr. Marchell Boston, Principal

"Mr. Andre Benito Mountain has engaged the community with his writings for over a decade. He has been featured in several notable publications addressing issues relating to youth education and educational leadership. He's an advocate for equity in education which is reflected through his writings. Mr. Mountain's writings come from an authentic lens of an African American principal's approach of what it's like to operate within the confines of an education system strife with oppression. I believe all readers and aspiring leaders will benefit from the experiences and obstacles Mr. Mountain has faced while confronting these challenges on a daily basis."

-Phillip Neely, Educator

"When André worked for the Richmond County School System the one aspect about him that always impressed me was his willingness to think outside the box. The Lucy Craft Laney Museum of Black History in Augusta, Georgia partnered with him to create a staff development day involving the 8th Grade Georgia History Instructors in the county. We began with an hour of instruction in the morning and that was the last time the educators were in a traditional classroom setting for the rest of the day. We set up field trips that lasted from 9:00 am to 4:00 pm. We took them to the various historic sites and museums all over the city. At the end of the session a veteran educator of over 30 years said, "I have never in all my 30 years of teaching history experienced a staff development day so enriching and engaging." It is that ability to go above and beyond to make the learning environment fun and exciting as well as educational and instructional. As I have gotten to know him it has become apparent to me that Andre has the creative gene and the energy to make education, no matter the level or age he is instructing, engaging."

-Corey Rogers, Museum Historian
Lucy Craft Laney Museum of Black History

"Over the past two years, I have not only gotten the chance to work, but to learn from Mr. Mountain. He is a man that is passionate about all things related to the education and the betterment of our students. He is a "Renaissance Man" in the way that he strives for greatness in the many endeavors he undertakes such as his tireless work as our principal, an accomplished author, an incredible facilitator and an advocate for unity. Mr. Mountain has the foresight and ability to lead Marbut through a global pandemic and a nation ripe with racial tension. He is the true embodiment of black excellence and a great role model to all of our students. To sum him up best, I will rely on Warren Buffet's quote, "Leadership is the capacity to translate vision into reality." This is who I am privileged to work with each day."

-Tanya Arrington, Educator

"André Benito Mountain is an innovative school leader who is deeply committed to improving the quality of education for Black and Brown children. He understands and advocates for the urgency of transformational change in our country's urban schools. His thought-provoking writings on school leadership and instruction is rooted in his success as a principal and teacher. During this time of racial justice advocacy and civil unrest, he is a calming and practical voice that needs to be heard. He is a black man, who has grown up in the black community, who has experienced the same challenges that many of our young people are currently handicapped by and has overcome those challenges to lead the educational development of students that reflect the younger version of who he once was. I know that Andre loves children and is deeply committed to support teachers in their work to properly educate today's students. In addition, I know that he is deeply concerned about educational inequities that result in the racial achievement gap and what is currently referred to as the school to-prison pipeline. Please hear this solution-oriented educator."

-Dr. Shango Blake, The Nations Hip Hop Principal

"Every now and then we are blessed to cross paths with someone you would never meet under normal circumstances, but that time happened when I was chosen by destiny to be in a group of outstanding teachers alongside André Benito Mountain. It was only after speaking with Mr. Mountain for a few minutes that I realized that although fate had made me a part of this young man's group, we were not equal in our God-given talents as educators. As I learned more and more about this amazing elementary school teacher, I found myself going ever deeper into a state of awe that one man was able to touch so many young lives in such a short period of time. He not only taught children every day during normal school hours, but he also worked in the poorest and neediest of neighborhoods in the area to make sure that every young child regardless of where he or she was would have access to learning support. He did not stop there. He took his natural-born ability to teach and to lead across the big pond so that others could see how even a single man's efforts can lead to change. Rarely is there a man or woman that can inspire so many through honest and unconditional love for children and learning but I am fortunate to have witnessed what this man has done over the past 20+ years and I am still in awe of his energy and undying support of not only children but also of adults who want to learn and make this world a better place for all through learning."

-Judy Hayward, Educator

"Working effectively in public schools requires an understanding of how a school acts as a hub of community and, being a dynamic leader who really gets this, makes Andre Benito Mountain a leader in education to follow and listen to. He has clearly gained great perspective from his journey in the educational sphere and his skill as a writer provides all of us the chance to be inspired by seeing what he sees, both what needs to be supported and grown and what needs to be changed. I have worked in partnership with Andre Benito Mountain from the time he was a fifth-grade teacher in Augusta, Georgia and we worked with his students to design and build a public art project for a park near his school. He demonstrated then that he knew the value of having students collaborate on projects that benefitted the community-at-large. Now that he been serving as a school principal, during my visits to his school and also reading his recent writing, it is clear that he is the kind of leader in education that we are especially in need of in this time of social upheaval as we struggle to uproot systemic racism. Andre is a visionary and I admire his stubbornness as he coaxes the best out of his teachers and their students and helps parents to see the importance of the choices they make. My frame of reference as a teaching artist, public artist, arts infusion specialist, and art for social justice activist also puts me squarely in Andre's corner. He understands how the arts engage students - and teachers - in the most powerful ways and instill an orientation towards creativity and problem solving that will lead them to make valuable contributions to their communities as they mature. "

-Jeff Mather, STEAM Teaching Artist, Public Artist

For my brother
Jeffrey Bertram Mountain,
Tierney Jean Akins
and the scholars of
Marbut Traditional Theme School

PRINCIPALS
DON'T
WALK
ON
WATER.

THEY WALK THROUGH IT.

ANDRÉ BENITO MOUNTAIN

Also by André Benito Mountain

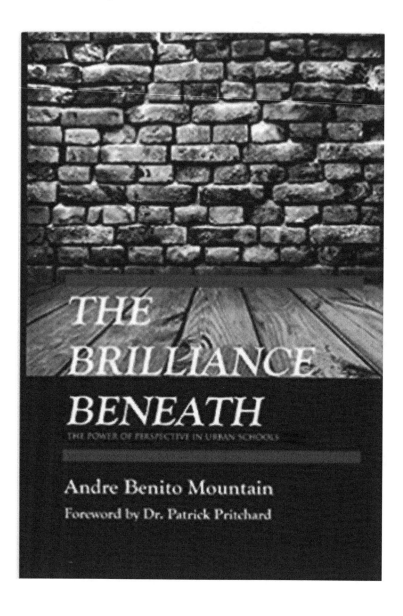

Also by André Benito Mountain

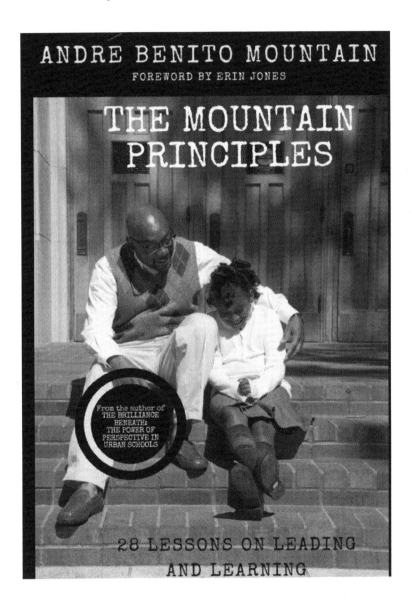

Def-Education LLC

Lithonia, Georgia

©2020 by André Benito Mountain

All rights reserved

ISBN: 9781711350875

Front cover photography by Melissa Alexander
https://www.phyllisiller.com/

About the Author photography by Ryan Manning

Back cover photography by William Mustafa
http://artworksofwilliammustafa.com/

Printed in the United States of America

WWW.DEF.EDUCATION

DEVELOP | ENGAGE | FLOURISH

We are all gifted, but we have to discover the gift,
uncover the gift, nurture and develop the gift,
and use it for the Glory of God and for the
liberation struggle of our people.

The Honorable Minister Louis Farrakhan

Acknowledgements

To my fallen heroes in the ongoing struggle for the liberation of Africans in the Americas: El-Hajj Malik El-Shabazz, Zora Neale Hurston, Dr. Martin Luther King, Jr., Shirley Chisolm, W.E.B. DuBois, Rosa Parks, Dr. Sebi, Harriet Tubman, Asa Hilliard, Mary Mcleod Bethune, Dr. William H. Watkins, Dr. Maya Angelou, Marva Collins, Fannie Lou Hamer, and Sojourner Truth.

To my wife Tanesha: When we met in downtown Augusta, I had no idea you lived across the street from the school where I was teaching. Thank you for being a source of inspiration and ideas as this book took shape. You posed the right questions and offered a balance of push-back and probing that took my thoughts to places I'd never imagined before. You've helped me think through complicated issues with a solid grounding in love for others and patience with myself. You remind me to look at events from all sides as a leader and to keep the big picture well in sight.

To my daughter Tierney: You are just an amazingly creative spark in our family. Having you as a student at our school for just two years was something I'd looked forward to. Seeing our school from the perspective and experience of my own daughter helped me to grow tremendously as a principal. It reminded me of what we must do to create spaces where students feel safe, loved, supported and challenged each day. You pushed through even when it wasn't easy. I see you reaching your goals and hope you continue to remain focused. There is no alternative to hard work and persistence. Success comes to those who go out and create it. You continue to challenge me on the tennis court and in Uno, but I'm going to keep coming for you!

To my parents Jimmie and Marie Mountain: Thank you for instilling a love for learning in me from an early age. I am who I am because of you. You both set a powerful example of consistent study, application of new learning and leadership. You've both been educators, entrepreneurs, and mentors for others. I hope that my journey into leadership. Mentorship, entrepreneurship and my ongoing scholarship shows you the legacy you created.

To my students at Marbut Traditional Theme School: Each day you teach me about tolerance, persistence, and unity. I am amazed at how you rise to exceed our expectations and express your love for learning and for the rich legacy of our school. Continue to walk into the legacy of greatness upon which our school design stands. Remember to stay positive, work hard, and make it happen. The world owes you nothing. Go out there and create.

There are several educators and artists who have been sources of information, guidance, and feedback as this book has taken shape. I would like to thank Derrick Brown, Dr. Marchell Boston, Rev. Glenn Harvey Andrews, Lucille Sharper, Lucille Patrick, Dr. Willie Adkinson, Dr. Emily Painter Driggers, Corey Washington, Bob Young, Dr. Sean Tartt, Christopher Brunson, C. Flux Sing, Pebbles the Artist, Amen Kush, Jason Louder, Jarrelle Evans, Ngoma Howard and Wayne Greer.

Thank you to the many faithful followers of my blog. Your feedback and discussions have helped the ideas in this book to develop further. I appreciate you. Special thanks to Tara Cleckley, Tanya Arrington, Jonie Lao, Nichelle Tanks, Tameka Lyseight, Camille Blakely, and Keenja Dennis.

To the DCSD family: Thanks for working alongside me as we create life-changing experiences for our scholars each day. This is the type of work that requires total commitment and you've shown that to me and our community each day. We may not walk on water each day, but we consistently make miracles happen for scholars and families each day. Your work does not go unnoticed. Thanks for giving your gifts to those who need them the most.

Author's Note

This is a work of nonfiction. There are no villains in this story, only aspiring heroes. This is not about placing blame upon anyone in the field of public education. To serve as an educator is to take on the mantle of a hero to someone. It may be a child, colleague, or a family who needs your support and guidance during a tough time. There are, however, folks who have inadvertently become the tools of the unseen hands that devise plans to undermine the education of many of our inner-city youth. There are exceptional days and there are days when everything seemingly falls apart. Principals aspire to serve as the gatekeepers for their respective schools and for the profession as a whole. We seek out candidates who show particular promise or commitment to the overall aims of our schools. This book provides a glimpse into those efforts and struggles. In most cases, I have tried to capture the complexity and curiosity that exists inside each of us. I have retold stories to the best of my recollection. There are no perfect schools, perfect districts, or perfect leaders. Principals do not walk on water. We are all seeking to become the best versions of ourselves. This work of counter-storytelling is my aspirational effort to humanize the work of the thousands of ambitious and committed school leaders. When possible, I have tried to provide rich and robust contexts for the events that have occurred. In some instances, names and locations have been changed to protect the privacy of the individuals referenced in the book.

Table of Contents

Preface

THE WRITING OF THIS BOOK CAME OUT OF A SET OF EXPERIENCES OVER THREE YEARS THAT fundamentally changed who I am as a man. The prologue to this story truly begins in Augusta, Georgia on the second floor of the district offices of the Richmond County School System where I had been serving as the K-12 social studies coordinator for 4 years. In supporting principals and their schools with assessments, resources, and instructional support, I gained a few wise mentors along the way. One of them, Mr. Glenn Andrews, would often visit my corner office when he came to the district offices for meetings or to drop off paperwork.

Glenn Andrews was an enigma of sorts. He was a highly successful principal at one of the district's most challenging middle schools. He'd developed more aspiring leaders under his leadership than any other principal in the district. He was not one to play politics or pandering. He was about the work and about helping kids and families and his work spoke for itself. He'd ease into my office with his trademark fedora in hand and trench coat draped across his forearm, sink comfortably into one of the leather chairs and say to me, "So when are you gonna get into a building Doc?" It was a question he'd posed to me at least half a dozen times. Each time my response was the same. "That's not what I'm trying to do right now." The truth is that I'd never seriously considered the idea of getting into school leadership because I loved the instructional side of teaching and curriculum work that I felt like the job of running a school would pull me away from those things I was most passionate about. I was naïve to think that the work of a principal is not truly immersed in curriculum, instruction, and assessment. Perhaps my perception of the work of a principal was based on an antiquated job description that has since changed. The principal of today must be the instructional leader in the building with the ability to deliver professional development, partner with members of the community to improve the overall school and delve into the assessment data to paint a realistic picture of where the school is going academically.

During my time as a curriculum coordinator, I began to take advantage of the opportunities to attend many educational conferences to expand my understanding of what was taking place in other districts in the area of Social Studies. While the district didn't always move with expediency in promoting talent within its ranks, I will say that they did a tremendous job of training their educators to the point that many of them were able to pursue successful opportunities in neighboring districts. This is something that I'd remember as I moved into school leadership roles later. Extensive professional development ideally should lead to opportunities to make additional contributions in other roles using that expertise in ways that drive student achievement. I wanted to know what innovative programs they were using and how they were assessing students. I believed that we could only move our teachers forward if we kept our fingers on the pulse of what was happening nationally and make intentional strides forward. During the conferences, I'd connect with other curriculum coordinators and pick their brains about what was working and how they were managing the work of leading the charge in larger school districts. I shared and I borrowed as much as I could. As a result, our Social Studies department saw considerable gains in student achievement as a result of some structural changes in how we delivered instruction, framed content, and focused on culturally relevant pedagogy. The gains in achievement were also the result of a set of visionary leaders within the district who saw the need to implement common assessments to monitor mastery throughout the year. While the implementation process encountered some resistance and missteps, the overall outcome was a change in the instructional culture of our department and increased accountability on all levels. These ongoing implementations, monitoring checks, and adjustments would shape my leadership lens for years to come and impact the decisions I'd make years later as a building principal.

　　　In late 2012, I was at a family function in Buford, Georgia, a suburb just north of Atlanta and began talking on the phone to an uncle who lived in Washington State. I told him that I'd been selected to present at the National Council for the Social Studies Conference that would be held in Seattle in November of 2012.

He urged me to consider visiting Tacoma and Puyallup during my visit. I agreed and ended up having a wonderful time seeing a part of the country that was previously unfamiliar to me. During the trip, his conversation to me was about becoming a school principal and using my knowledge of curriculum and instruction to push a school forward. It reminded me of the conversations I'd been having with Mr. Andrews back in Augusta. Again, it was something I wasn't too interested in, but as I explored the innovative programs in the districts in the Pacific Northwest, my mind began to slowly open up to the idea of joining the ranks of school leadership. I began reading about the state-wide push in Washington to support social-emotional learning. I knew that this was the missing piece in many schools that allowed many trauma-affected students to fall through the cracks because teachers and administrators lacked the resources or training to provide what families needed. I was also very impressed by what I saw in the way of diversity and equity work taking place in the Pacific Northwest. Schools are the frontlines of the racial and economic disparities that exist in our communities. Even in 2013, this was still an extremely tough discussion to have in the American South, and the Pacific Northwest was at least making a valiant attempt to engage administrators and educators in the discussion with committees and book studies to peel away the layers of institutional bias that have been a part of public education since its inception. The more I read, the more I began to see myself as a potential school leader given the right supports and mentorship.

In 2013, the curriculum team I was working with attended the Harvard Graduate School of Education's Instructional Rounds Institute in Cambridge, Massachusetts. During the program, we worked in conjunction with other school leaders and teams from around the country to help schools in Boston strategize solutions to their problem of practice. We visited Edison Elementary in Boston and observed multiple classrooms. The experience helped me to understand what high-quality instruction looks like and how school leaders address instructional concerns with systems and approaches to home in on a specific problem of practice. The time at Harvard planted seeds that would emerge when I began working as a school administrator in Washington State in 2014.

When you read the title "Principals Don't Walk on Water", my hope is that you get a sense of the unrealistic expectations that are often thrust upon school leaders. It should hint at the notion that we are human beings, prone to mistakes and missteps. Please don't place us on a pedestal because we've chosen to devote our lives to creating spaces where children learn to read, write and do mathematics. We still get angry, have disappointments, and fall short in various aspects of our lives. I can recall getting stopped by police for making an illegal turn on a one-way street. Surrounded by police officers on a metro-Atlanta street, I seemingly answered the same questions over and over. I eventually received a ticket for reckless driving, paid a fine, and served one year on probation. For a year I balanced the irony of leading a staff at my school and then reporting to the probation office to pay a portion of my fine and confirm that I hadn't gotten in any additional mischief. The probation office would be packed with other African-Americans complaining about missing work, making their probation payments and the potential of violating their probation if they were unable to pay the monthly fee. There were women holding infants and elderly people all caught up in the matrix of non-violent offenses. Here I was, principal of a school checking in each month with my assigned officer. In retrospect, it was an opportunity for me to see what life is like for a large segment of the population that does not have the luxury of returning to an office and a salaried position with a retirement plan. It was a humbling experience that brought an awareness of our criminal justice system that I had not experienced firsthand. I came to see the prison-industrial complex for what it was. I became intimately aware of the monetary incentives that fueled mass incarceration for non-violent offenders. While the reckless driving experience reignited my desire to create spaces that nurture and develop youth to think critically and become forces of change in their communities, it had a different impact on others. Despite the facts of the traffic stop, some zealous members of my school community, particularly those who were looking for any way to discredit my work as a leader, went into action to recategorize my reckless driving ticket as a ticket for driving under the influence. Folks printed my driving record and showed it to parents as though they were campaigning for an election. It was funny, because I'd never even seen my own driving record. As the rumors continued to spread, I had to report to work each day knowing the truth, but also knowing that I had a job to do. Maya Angelou once said, "When people show you who they are, believe them." After being shown, I made a mental note and continued with the tasks at hand. Eventually the truth prevailed, and the focus returned to the work we were doing with young people. I want to ignite that same fervor into spreading the word about our fundraising efforts for our urban garden or for our campus beautification work. How much better would our schools be if we spread the news about an upcoming board meeting and the need for us to show up to champion a cause on behalf of our students? At the last PTA meeting of 2019-2020 we had only 6% of our parents present at the meeting. That means that 94% of the potential attendees were not present for our PTA meeting. Truth be told, we were in the midst of a global pandemic and this was our first virtual PTA meeting. Still, I was disappointed that the turnout was so low and made it a point to thank the attendees who logged on for being there at such a critical moment. My point here is that the tremendous work of schools can't rest solely on the shoulders of principals. Principals must have the support and cooperation of their staff and families to get great work accomplished.

I consider myself fortunate to be in a school district that understands the many layers of support that principals need to get this work accomplished. Upon arriving in Dekalb, I was assigned a skillful mentor, Dr. Linda Priester, who was a successful veteran principal. She worked closely with me and another early career principal. Our school designs were very similar, so she was instrumental in helping me understand how to communicate the high expectations to parents and staff, and more importantly, how to enforce those high expectations on a daily basis. Not only did she call me frequently to check on how I was doing, Dr. Priester would occasionally stop by and sit in on my strategic planning sessions with my leadership team. She became extended family as she posed solutions to the questions we had and helped us to think through how we would address chronic late arrivals of scholars and repeat discipline offenses.

The other layer of support they provided was the induction into a cohort of new principals with assigned Performance Coaches who were retired administrators. My performance coach, Mrs. Lucille Sharper, was critical to my survival and my sanity during the first three years of my principalship. She visited the school at minimum every two weeks and sat in when I had critical meetings with staff, parents, and sometimes as I interviewed teaching candidates. Her insight into the day-to-day challenges of running a school helped me realize that I wasn't losing my mind at times. She shared ideas from other schools and borrowed ideas from our school to support other principals.

The support I received is what I hope every emerging school leader is afforded because the responsibilities of school leadership are expansive. I'm forever grateful to these women who were patient enough to answer may many questions, loyal enough to allow me to vent, and wise enough to allow me to make just enough mistakes that I learned the right leadership lessons along the way. Thanks to them, I've been able to walk through some of the most turbulent waters.

Foreword by Ngoma Howard

"When you walk through the fire, you will not be burned;
the flames will not set you ablaze."
Isaiah 43:2

Hope

It was a warm August morning and the non-airconditioned room at the professional development complex was already stuffy. Motivational feel-good music pulsated through the air to calm nerves and set a tone of optimism. As I scanned the room looking for a familiar face in the sea of administrators both green and seasoned, all I could think about is "How will I make my mark today?" I felt like a new student in a new school with peers that were my colleagues and, in some cases, unknowing foes. The room was teeming with energy, anxiety and overwhelming optimism as a new academic year had arrived. This atmosphere is paralleled by many others all over the country where administrators congregate to learn, strategize and motivate one another for the journey ahead.

The interplay between leaders, aspiring leaders, and those there to support them was drenched in social agreements and an established order. Throughout history, we have seen this play out many times. Every tribe has a leadership structure rooted in social agreements based on common values and rituals. We can look back at historic biblical accounts of prophets who possess a message for the masses who sojourned for years under their guidance in the ultimate search for wisdom. As such, we gather annually in somewhat tribal yet biblical fashion looking to our leaders for guidance, wisdom eventually being anointed principals as followers who will, in turn, become symbolic prophets to our staff students, and community.

Disciples

During this symbolic meeting, I met and got to know André Benito Mountain. A charismatic yet humble man who flashed hints of brilliance when he spoke while contributing to personal and or open group dialogue. I knew I was in the presence of an extremely gifted colleague. In a room full of may accomplished individuals, André did his best to keep his eyes and ears open as did I because we were the few, the others. A few of the assistant principals made up a small but significant part of the African American leadership. As with most social constructs, particularly the African American culture, an instant bond was formed among this group. Although the bond was unspoken, it was clear and predestined as though it was a part of our cultural DNA.

As my connection with André grew, I found myself alongside a comrade who not only shared a mutual love of learning and leadership but would one day become a star in our ranks. Little did we both know that such destinies were not in our hands. Now I would like to say that we both went on to have incredible years. However, this would be the beginning of a long and arduous initiation into the cultural and racial red tape and blurred lines of inequity that plague and stifle black and brown, male and female upward trajectories and success in this country.

Fear and blurred lines

As with any high stakes industry, missteps can mean major setbacks which impact bottom lines. In public education, where funding is tied to progress guided by uniform standards that apply to all, one's career trajectory is and will be positively or adversely impacted. Here is the rub! Who you are, what you look like are not purported to be factored in this outcome, however, nothing could be further from the truth. There is this perception in diverse communities that because we are so diverse, we are excused from the presumptions of bias and racism because it doesn't exist here. One of the issues people of color have is being appointed to a leadership position on merit but then being expected to lead in a fashion that resembles the status quo. The typically unspoken expectation lingers in the air that one is only a symbolic leader filling a slot of a pre-determined role. Andre and I found this to go against everything we knew and stood for. This was the grim reality of administrative leadership that was only whispered about in corners after meetings and professional development sessions. Small groups of African American educators found themselves lamenting about this regularly. We sought solace and understanding in each other's experiences to maintain our confidence. We began to doubt our abilities, and this negatively affected our decision-making when it came to key issues that impacted, staff, student and communities. This leads to false perceptions from directors and other district supervisors.

The Way Forward

Being a principal is an enormous responsibility and has many challenges. Being an African American principal carries an additional layer. The unspoken layer of "I must be even better than the best" to be seen or accepted as sufficient. That's why this book is so important it gives us yet another perspective into the African American principal experience. Many of us know of the boldly spoken criticisms principals already received from some staff and families. It is also common to hear the sentiment which is overwhelmingly popular with some White teachers who think they can do a better job than the African American principals they already have. These are some of the stark reminders of how our country's ugly past continues to have strong roots that drive race perceptions and behaviors.

Even with these obstacles, André was and continues to be a force of relentless conviction and character. He has masterfully channeled his background in jazz and instructional leadership into his work and began transforming his school using his now highly acclaimed Mountain Principles. Those principles were formulated out of his work and cultivated at in one of the most ethnically diverse schools in the Pacific Northwest. Despite his tireless work, André was still being overlooked for promotions. The message was received loud and clear. It is fair to say that André was not seen as a building principal rather a solid assistant. This experience was destined and is responsible for the transformation we have seen into one of the prescient educational voices of our time. After prayer and consultation with trusted friends and confidants, André drew on his faith and paved an unknown path that would lead him forward. As with all successful journey's, he had a vision, and the courage to forge ahead. You see as André once told me, " I will write my own story."

Redemption

In this book "Principals Don't Walk on Water – They Walk Through It", he draws from his faith in the ideas of leadership and how they parallel society's view of school principals. The prophet-like symbolism that society not only craves but needs to maintain order in this social agreement that we refer to as a society is present in this book. The collective feeling of hope and the symbolism of disciples who battle the fear of not knowing what our future holds for our children, and community is present in this book.

As principals, we don't walk on water but as effective leaders, we are looked at and given the power, faith, and perception that we can not only walk on water but also move mountains. I hope that this book further illuminates your path as you find your way on your journey.

Ngoma Howard, Educator
August 2020

"I am just one of the people who is sick of the social order, sick of the establishment, sick to my soul of it all. To me, America's society is nothing but a cancer, and it must be exposed before it can be cured. I am not the doctor to cure it. All I can do is expose the sickness."

- Nina Simone

Chapter 1: "Swingin' in the Southern Breeze"

Corporal Punishment in Georgia Schools: 20-2-730, et seq. It may not be excessive or unduly severe or be used as a first line of punishment; it must be administered in the presence of a school official; a written explanation must be provided on request; and it may not be administered if a physician certifies that the child's mental or emotional stability could be affected.

N 1962, A BRISK AUTUMN HAD FALLEN UPON TENNILLE, GEORGIA'S D.D. CRAWFORD SCHOOL. IT WAS AN ALL-BLACK ELEMENTARY SCHOOL DURING THE YEARS BEFORE SCHOOL INTEGRATION THAT STOOD ON A STREET THAT WOULD LATER BE RENAMED AFTER DR. MARTIN LUTHER KING, JR, A CHAMPION OF NON-VIOLENCE. The math teacher, Mr. Dennis, was a beacon in the community. He and all of the teachers at the school were looked up to as respectable professionals who'd come back to help educate the youth of one of the state's poorest rural communities. On this morning, he had asked the class to produce their homework from the night before. The room grew still with silence. As he waited for the students to pull the papers from their desks and bags, his anger smoldered because it appeared that the entire class had not done the assignment. He slammed his hand against the oak desk, "Everybody outside now!" The class of thirty-five black children, mostly from sharecropping families one generation removed from slavery, quickly filed out of the classroom. Mr. Dennis grabbed his wooden paddle and looked at the students over his glasses with a look of disbelief. "I gave this assignment and I expected it to be completed. Unacceptable! This is what happens when you don't follow directions. Everybody has to pay the consequences now." One by one, Mr. Dennis struck each student twice on the buttocks with the wooden paddle that had been used as his primary means of behavior management since the start of his teaching career. Just the sound of the blows was intimidating. Mr. Dennis poured his frustration into each swing of the wooden board. Next in line was Jim, a skinny fourteen-year-old kid whose family grew vegetables in on a plot of land not too far from the school. Jim loved school and read voraciously. Jim actually had his homework in his desk. He thought, "Should I tell him?" Jim was hesitant because he didn't want to be the only student in the class who produced the homework and risk being the brunt of jokes from his classmates. He placed his hands against the wall, took the two blows, and returned to his seat. Once he walked back into the classroom, Jim quietly lifted the top of his wooden desk, reached for the homework, folded it neatly and placed it in the pocket of his overalls.

What Jim experienced is not unlike the violence inflicted upon Black bodies across the American South during the 60's. The fear of violence against Black bodies at the hands of racists and law enforcement, dominated all aspects of life. The inflicting of pain upon the bodies of children at the hands of school officials was state sanctioned with laws that are still in place today. Both Mr. Dennis and Jim were positioned in an oppressive system that perpetuated this devaluing of the complex inner-workings of Black life, strivings, and the psychology of fear. Jim would later attend Fort Valley State College and become an educator. Jim's experience would have implications for my own journey as an educator. Jim is my father.

THE YEAR WAS 1963. BLACK COLLEGE STUDENTS AND CIVIL RIGHTS ACTIVISTS FILLED THE STREETS OF BIRMINGHAM IN ORGANIZED NON-VIOLENT PROTESTS. BLACK COLLEGE STUDENTS CONDUCTED SIT-INS AT LUNCH COUNTERS WAITING FOR SERVICE THAT NEVER CAME BECAUSE OF THE COLOR OF THEIR SKIN. During that same month, about four hours east of Birmingham, Marie was a ninth grader at T.J. Elder High School staging a silent protest of her own. It was a warm Spring day in 1963, a perfect backdrop for a day away from classes. She and her sister Helen had decided that they would arrive at school but cut classes for most of the day. The plan was to meet in the restroom, wait for the bell to ring, and then to casually walk off campus and spend the day at the park. The bell rang and they could hear the hallways clearing out as everyone reported to their homeroom classes.

Marie waited inside the restroom stall until she heard the familiar footsteps of the school principal, Mr. Taylor. His wingtips made an unmistakable sound as they tapped against the hard tile floors. His gait was slow, deliberate and recognizable. She quickly stood on the top of the toilet so that he would not be able to see her black and white saddle oxfords. The stall door suddenly flew open and there stood the school principal staring at her through thick horn-rimmed glasses.

"And what are you doing young lady?", he asked.

"I...I was gonna go to class, but I needed some more time", she said.

"You realize, don't you, that this won't end well for you. Report to the office Marie. Now." he said. His voice hinted at his growing agitation that she would try to not only skip classes but convince him that she was not up to something. She stepped down from the toilet, grabbed her stack of books and marched through the empty halls toward the office. Mr. Taylor presented her with two options. The first option was for him to place a call to her parents to notify them that she was sneaking around the school and not in classes. She knew that her parents would be furious, and the consequences would be severe when she returned home that evening. The second option he presented was that she would receive a paddling and return to class. It's not that she didn't care, but she knew that both options would lead to physical pain. But she absolutely knew that the severity of the blows inflicted by her principal would not compare to the blows at the hands of her mother.

"I'll take the paddling! Just don't tell my mama." she pleaded.

Mr. Taylor already knew which option she would choose. He'd seen this scenario play out hundreds of times before with other students. He reached down, opened the bottom drawer of his desk and pulled out a wooden paddle inscribed with the words "Board of Education". It was a sinister nod to the power of the wooden board to correct the wrongs of pupils with just a brief but 'impactful' appearance. After her meeting with the "Board of Education" Marie made her way to class and never uttered a word about what had happened in the restroom or the office. Marie would later become a teacher. Marie is my mother.

Some twenty years after my parents had their respective experiences with corporal punishment in Georgia schools, I would sit in a classroom at Swainsboro, Georgia and again bear witness to the pervasive belief that beatings in schools were an effective method for controlling behavior. Interestingly though, by 1983 my schools was an integrated school. The principal, Mr. Crenshaw, was White and the assistant principal, Mr. Eason, was Black. Mr. Eason was the "muscle" around the school. I'd witnessed him march many students out of class, into the hallway and inflict several loud blows with a thick wooden paddle. The familiar sound of the board making contact with an unlocking soul would echo down the hallways. Interestingly though, I never saw him paddle a White child. There was either a stark difference in how discipline was prescribed for them or he wisely adhered to an unwritten rule about who could and couldn't be the recipients of his "board of education".

In 2004 I was a 5th grade teacher at Jessie Rice Elementary in Macon, Georgia. Nigel had interrupted my class for the last time. I wrote him up and sent the referral to the office. The principal called back to the classroom and told me to bring Nigel to her office during his P.E. time. I imagined she was going to call his parents and have him spend a few days at home. When we walked into her office she was standing in front of her desk. She looked at him and told him that he was not here to disrupt the learning of others. She told him that she was not going to tolerate his behavior any longer. She turned around, picked up a wooden board from her desk and told him to bend over the desk. Then she delivered three swift blows to Nigel as I looked on. I recall the times I'd heard that sound coming from the hallways of my elementary school, but this time I was actually seeing it firsthand as a result of a referral I wrote. I was an accessory to this crime. In an almost methodical manner, she passed me a clipboard to sign that I had witnessed the paddling. I signed and walked back to class with Nigel. I didn't know what to say. There were no words. I didn't intend for him to get beaten as a result of my referral. But I didn't say anything. Neither did he. I never wrote another student up during my time at Jessie Rice. I learned to manage my classroom discipline without involving the school administration. This may have been the moment when I unconsciously decided that becoming a principal was not in my future. I wondered if she had received training on delivering the blows without causing injury. Was there a certain protocol to determine when she would paddle and when she would use other methods. It all seemed so barbaric to me. Discipline like this, if administered at all, should be done by parents, not by educators. My principal at Jessie Rice was very likely a product of the same structures for managing behavior that my parents were nurtured in at D.D. Crawford School and T.J. Elder School. While discipline was important, this brutal method didn't sit well with me.

There are 19 states in which corporal punishment is still legal. Those states are Alabama, Arkansas, Arizona, Colorado, Florida, Georgia, Idaho, Indiana, Kansas, Kentucky, Louisiana, Missouri, Mississippi, North Carolina, Oklahoma, South Carolina, Tennessee, Texas, and Wyoming. While only about 15% of Georgia's schools report that they continue to use this practice, it is interesting that the states where corporal punishment is still legal predominately consists of former slave-holding states who were part of the Confederacy. This assault on the bodies of children, particularly Black children, is part of a long legacy that lingers on the pages of school laws.

Today the way that law is enforced in African American communities reminds me of how brutality has been a familiar foe in our lives in this country. Brutality that existed in the larger society found a place in our schools. Now, we see the outgrowth of that same brutality, that belief that violence inflicted upon a person will instill enough fear in others that behavior will be managed through psychological intimidation. This is the mindset that made lynching in the American South a social occasion documented in photographs depicting celebratory crowds. The public nature of the brutality was intended to send a message to others of what their fate might be if they did not adhere to the social order in place.

I am thankful to work as a principal during a time when members of the education profession have developed a deeper understanding of the intricacies of trauma, research on the social-emotional aspects of education, and the importance of relationships in creating successful student outcomes. Educators are more aware of how disparities can emerge to undermine opportunities for students of color as they find themselves on the disproportionate end of corporal punishments, school suspensions, and expulsions. I'm equally hopeful that the way Black bodies are perceived by law enforcement in our communities continues to evolve beyond the brutality that we see on our streets today. Dozens of examples of unarmed African-American men and women whose interactions with law enforcement have left their "Black bodies hanging in the Southern breeze" for us to see as monuments of our ongoing oppression. Principals have an opportunity to push against this narrative in the ways they educate students, train teachers, and inflict discipline in their schools. The opportunity to enact social justice in school has never been more important than right now in 2020. Teachers need comprehensive training on mentoring, restorative discipline practices and the disproportionality that exists when it comes to suspensions among African-American boys and students with disabilities. Pressures to implement zero tolerance policies come from parents and teachers. Narratives are spun to characterize more informed approaches to discipline as "being soft" on students. The waters are troubled and deep, but courageous principals are walking through it each day.

WALKING THROUGH ATLANTA'S LITTLE FIVE POINTS NEIGHBORHOOD IS A SATURDAY RITUAL FOR ME. From Moreland Avenue, I find my usual table in the corner of Sevananda Natural Foods Market and observe the steady flow of eclectic patrons pouring into the iconic store. I've been visiting Sevananda since the early 90's and the experience has always been the same. Every staff member greets me as if they have known me for years. Like Apple and Starbucks, Sevananda has mastered the art of emotional intelligence in a truly organic way to make customers feel welcomed and appreciated. Schools and organizations aspire for success. But when it comes to success, we have to make sure we are using the same metrics to determine what it means to be successful. For schools, success can either mean a great learning experience, effective resources, increasingly positive student outcomes, or high levels of structure and order. Success when seen through the lens of a school principals isn't solely about scores, scales and percentiles. The notion of success goes much deeper than most would imagine when you peel away the layers of emotional intelligence at work in schools. Teachers and students are dealing with issues of trauma. This is coupled with the interactions with parents who, with the best intentions, come into some meetings with a confrontational approach. Learning to diffuse those moments is the critical skill that one must have to survive in the role. So what does are some of the components of success? The success of the school also depends heavily on people skills and positive interactions that occur within its walls daily. Hiring and retaining staff with high levels of emotional intelligence and maturity is critical to the success of any business or brand.

Barack Obama was a master of demonstrating emotional intelligence. As president, he understood the impact of small gestures in conveying humility and empathy. Several years ago, I read about the handwritten notes then President Obama would write to people thanking them for their letters and encouragement. What a great way to connect with people and show them that their voices matter. In seeing the dedication of my faculty and staff, I've taken it upon myself to borrow this approach, making more time this year to write personal, handwritten acknowledgements of their outstanding efforts to create an amazing learning environment for our kids. Taking the time to handwrite these notes is a pause in my day to focus on the positive efforts of my team. Helping others to see that their efforts haven't gone unnoticed is one way of conveying empathy and strengthening collective commitment to a common cause.

As an elementary administrator, I can recall a school secretary at Larchmont Elementary in Tacoma, WA who radiated positivity and demonstrated a high degree of emotional intelligence in her role. Mrs. Artero greeted every customer as if they'd been childhood friends. In every problem she saw a solution and worked to show compassion about a sick or injured child or a death in a family. She set the tone for all of the interactions in the school because hers was the first interaction. Never did we receive a complaint about her customer service because she understood that her role was not to win arguments, but to win over customers. She understood the cardinal rule of interactions: first impressions matter more than any others.

He was 9 years old and it was his first year at our school. I'd heard his name mentioned several times as "one to watch" in 4th grade. "Kase". I kept hearing this name and seeing this name on discipline referrals. It was a Friday afternoon and I saw a commotion in the cafeteria. I approached 5 students and asked, "What's going on?". Everyone got silent. One laughed. I asked, "What's your name?" He said, "Kase". Ah...it was my first encounter with the new scholar. He continued laughing. I asked him to come with me. He refused. I asked him to come with me two more times. He refused. Finally, I told him that refusing to comply with an adult request is not acceptable. He could either come with me or end up with a more severe consequence for non-compliance. Once in my office I began explaining to Kase that I've been hearing his name and reading the discipline referrals about his behavior in class. I explained that I was going to call his mother and we would have to discuss next steps. I immediately called his mom and she said that she would be at the school in ten minutes. It seemed more like five minutes and she was in my office with her hands in his chest saying "What is this about? Huh?" She asked him to wait outside as we talked. Tearfully, she went on to explain how she'd endured years of domestic violence and that Kase had been a witness to much of it at the hands of his father. She shared experiences of living out of her car, losing everything, and rebuilding over time. She talked about how she prayed that he could attend a school like ours and what this meant to her and to him. She shared that he had expressed feeling rage and having nightmares. I suggested that she look into family counseling as a way to confront the many emotions swirling within her and within Kase. Our task as a school is to identify families and students like Kase who need support and connect them with resources to address the mental health issues that impede learning and healing. The obsession with test scores and school ratings misses this key factor that determines student and school success.

Looming Storm Clouds

The "Kases" of the world eventually become adults. Is there someone on your job who is constantly in conflict with people? Is there a customer who visits your business and always has a complaint about the service? You ask yourself, "Why do they continue to return to an establishment where they can't seem to find anything that meets their standards of excellence?" Why do they continue to do a job that they obviously loathe? Working in public education brings me in contact with many interesting personalities. I find that many of the people I encounter who seem to have chaotic lives lack emotional intelligence. The spiral of conflict is not isolated to their workplace. It is pervasive like a cancer in every aspect of their lives. The last year is a graveyard of their burned relationships and interactions. Wherever they go, storm clouds seem to loom overhead, pulling innocent bystanders into the perpetual storms that follow these unfortunate souls. Some roles, where interactions with the public are paramount for the successful branding of the company, require even higher levels of emotional intelligence. So, what is it?

Emotional Intelligence Defined

Emotional intelligence includes self-awareness, managing emotions, showing empathy, and learning the arts of cooperation. I've witnessed firsthand members of my team who have mastered the art of cooperation and customer service. It seems innate to them because they truly understand and love interacting with people. Mrs. Crowe-Harris is an example of an educator who just gets it when it comes to interacting with the public. By day she is a highly regarded classroom teacher whose reputation is such that parents request and demand that their children be placed in her classroom based on the accounts of other parents. In the afternoon, she transitions to the role of the director of our after-school program. With finesse, she changes from the role of the classroom teacher to a teacher leader managing customer service, payroll, payments, and parent concerns. She is able to navigate the emotional gauntlet of showing empathy, holding people accountable, and not taking things personally. From my office I can hear her skillfully deescalating a potential problem by saying, "Ok Mom, here is what happened…Now, this is what we are going to do because we have made it very clear to him what the expectation is…" Parents can't help but respect that level of emotional fortitude and empathy.

In my book, The Mountain Principles: The Power of Perspective in Urban Schools, I wrote about my experience at the barbershop Groomzmen on Euclid Avenue in Atlanta. The way the barbers connect with their customers is essential to their business model. The conversation, the attention to detail, and the willingness to invest time into building trust matter in successful businesses.

What is it about people like Mrs. Artero, Mrs. Crowe-Harris and the barbers at Groomzmen that sets them apart from others who lack emotional intelligence? They understand that people are coming from a wide range of emotional perspectives. Customers want to be made to feel welcomed and understood. Customers want to interact with people who possess the emotional maturity to know that every comment or action is not a personal attack. Employees with emotional intelligence understand how to balance holding others and themselves accountable. They are able to convey empathy because being emotionally intelligent human being means putting your own ego aside most of the time. On the other hand, people who lack emotional intelligence seem to find fault with everyone else. When communication goes haywire, it's always someone else's fault. Even when they receive the same feedback from family, friends, and supervisor, they are unable to take any ownership of the issue.

During the summer of 2019, all of the principals in our district attended a Summer Leadership Retreat where the focus was on Mental Health Awareness. The sessions all centered around the mental health issues that permeate urban communities. There is so much trauma that funnels into the doors of urban schools on Monday mornings.

- A mother shares that her son never gets to spend time with his father. The father makes promises and never keeps them. At school the boy acts out his aggression on his classmates and his teacher.
- A staff member gets little attention from her spouse and arrives at work displaying attention-seeking behaviors to any males who pass her by: teachers, parents, and visitors.
- A teacher feels unfulfilled in her role as a classroom teacher. Her passions lie elsewhere. When confronted with

feedback on her mediocre efforts in the classroom she lashes out and becomes defensive and unprofessional.

Cowardly Aggression

As a principal, the challenge that presents itself in the course of a school day is to maintain a focus on instruction. In recent years, managing the emotional struggles of adults has become a more pressing matter to preserve a positive school culture in a world where drama and controversy seem to be the focal point of entertainment outlets. This trauma stems from issues of abandonment, witnessing physical and emotional abuse, and lack of self-esteem and self-determination. If one feels powerless in society, they may adopt a defensive perspective about all interactions, even when there is no attack to defend against. Perpetual conflict with others may stem from a lack of self-esteem and self-confidence. In an effort to refine our school's approach to customer service, I sent out a survey to parents about ways we might improve customer service. For the first few days, great responses were rolling in with very constructive feedback about where we might improve. Then, after a few days, the commentary devolved into profanity laced ramblings about isolated events and personal misgivings about specific people. I closed the survey because the platform was becoming a sounding board for the emotionally immature. It's unfortunate that even when given an opportunity to add value to our institutions, actions suggesting a lack of emotional intelligence undermine authentic dialogue. Somewhere along the way we've lost our respect for civil and productive dialogue. I believe that the anonymity of email and message boards has fueled a cowardly aggression where people say things that they know are out of bounds in these electronic spaces because they lack the emotional intelligence to provide constructive solutions to the problems they encounter in life. Removing the stigma around mental health in the African American community is a step forward. These actions are cries for help from our community.

The book *"Emotional Intelligence: Why it can matter more than IQ"* by Daniel Goleman explains the roots of the development of our emotional intelligence. He writes, "By fourth and fifth grade, as peer relationships take on an immense importance in their lives, they get lessons that help their friendships work better: empathy, impulse control, and anger management." As a father of a 6th grader, I'm constantly watching and observing how she handles relationships with her peers, responds to disagreements, and manages friendships. How can I be a better father in the area of supporting her emotional intelligence? Ongoing conversations about how to handle conflict are taking place in our household. Most importantly, she is observing how my wife and I work through problems, reach compromises, and move forward after disagreements.

I.Q. matters.

Black Lives Matter.

But Emotional Intelligence matters too!

No matter how hard reality seems

Just hold on to your dreams

Don't give up and don't give in

Although it seems you never win

You will always pass the test

As long as you keep your head to the sky

You can win as long as you keep your head to the sky

You can win as long as you keep your head to the sky

Be optimistic

-Sounds of Blackness

The Phoenix Must Burn

According to Arabian legend, the phoenix is a bird that burns itself every 500 years, then, miraculously, emerges from those ashes to live for another 500-year span. The legend goes on to state that only one phoenix lived at a time and the burning and emergence was a renewal process. In order for many of us to emerge from our failure and stumbles, we have to burn away some of the chafe that held us down in the first place. I see a distinct difference between those who are especially effective and those who flounder and struggle professionally. The difference is the pool from which they draw their counsel and advice in critical professional and personal moments. Be careful about the pools from which you chose to drink. There are refreshing streams, stagnant puddles, raging rivers, and peaceful ponds. We are **what** we listen to AND we become like those **to whom we listen**. Persistent pessimism breeds more of the same and looks for a challenge in every opportunity. Persistent optimism and relentless hope will get you through the toughest times.

In life we don't always get to choose our teachers. Our teachers may choose us to teach us the lessons that universe knows we must learn to move forward. Often people with experience, education, or other credentials find it awkward to learn from those who are less experienced, less credentialed or younger than they are. "What can I learn from him?" *Neither age and nor tenure in a teaching position are guarantees of effectiveness, wisdom or emotional maturity.* Generational tension can arise in teams simply due to the span of ages that are present and the different perspectives on how the workplaces should operate and who should have specific roles can become a sticking point. Rebecca Knight writes about this in her article Managing People from 5 Generations in the Harvard Business Review. But the humility to add to one's tool kit with wisdom and information from the newest employee on the team, or a younger colleague could be the key to getting you to the next level of productivity in your work. I borrowed an idea from the volunteer coordinator at Atlanta's Fernbank Museum. A skilled non-profit executive, she uses an online sign-up system to coordinate volunteers for the museum. As a principal at a school whose parents are required to complete volunteer hours, I've been looking for a software to assign specific roles to volunteers and minimize idle time and duplication of tasks. A savvy 20-something

ATlien led me to a solution that has brought our school into the 21st century of volunteer management.

If you are fortunate enough to have people around you who are courageous enough to tell you when you've floundered in some area, you are truly blessed. I'd imagine that truth serum is bitter, because telling close friends the truth when they ask your opinion can be a bitter moment indeed. The sweet taste of reaffirming words lifts the responsibility from us and places it on the villain. The antagonist suddenly becomes the person who must change while we remain as we always have been. Wise counsel guides us toward the mirror of self-reflection. As we walk, we live wide awake seeking for opportunities to grow and evolve along the way. Some people don't want to wake up from their own reality to see a situation for what it is. Changing one's approach after self-reflection, can be one of the most difficult things to do. Pride, ego and our self-image are enshrouded in cases that grow stronger as we spend years without friends willing to chip away at the hardened bark and roots that form.

For the last year, my mantra as a principal has been: Stay positive. Work hard. Make it happen. These are three simple phrases that any age can relate to. The first phrase is key because it sets the tone for what we see, feel, and hear throughout the day. The moment darkness enters our realm as a teacher, or school leader, we have to drive it out with the light of persistent optimism and relentless hope. We are what we listen to. Whether it's music, friends, or sermons...we tend to live and pursue that which is poured into us. It's easy to identify that one interaction of the day that went awry, but there were 600 other interactions that went smoothly. Which one will resonate in your mind on the way home?

Recommendations

Retraining the mind, with the guidance of the Critical Friends process, we can all improve the quality of our professional practice by getting the constructive feedback we often need to see our work from the outside in. Given the events of 2020 in the wake of the Covid-19 global pandemic, school principals all over the country will need to make social emotional learning a priority for their schools. This means that in addition to creating structures for virtual or hybrid learning during this instructional shift, they need to also consider how to leverage members of their team to mentor and attend to the social-emotional needs of families. The abrupt end of the 2019-2020 school year and separation from friends and trusted adults will need to be addressed. Those feelings inside of our kids will need to be unpacked during virtual morning meetings of small group counseling sessions. We have work to do with the emotions of our young people before we return to the work of educating them about content.

We need to make sure families are safe and secure during this time when many parents may have lost their primary sources of income. This is the time to introduce life skills classes and to promote restorative practices in the home and at school. There are many families who struggle to provide healthy meals each day for their households. Schools need to tap into their community partners including the faith community, non-profits, and corporations that benefit from the communities we serve. There are families in need and the school principal is there to be the intermediary between those who need and those who can serve those needs.

Chapter 2: Brackish Water

"Not many of you should become teachers, my fellow believers, because you know that we who teach will be judged more strictly."
James 3:1

TAKING ON A LEADERSHIP ROLE MEANS YOU MUST QUICKLY GAIN THE TOLERANCE FOR BRACKISH WATER. Brackish waters are those waters with a mixture of freshwater and saltwater. Only certain animal and plant life can survive in brackish waters. If you place any organism in brackish waters that must have freshwater or saltwater, they will quickly expire due to the harsh conditions of the water. Brackish waters tend to be a bit salty.

When I appeared on the Next Level Teaching Podcast with Jeremy Anderson in July 2020, I shared for the first time how the title of this book came into being. One particular morning at Marbut Traditional Theme School helped me to gain a better understanding of what it means to walk through brackish waters. I arrived at the school and immediately noticed that there were many more students than usual in the cafeteria. I looked around the lobby and the staff seemed to be flustered. The kids were getting impatient and I began asking staff why so many students were still in the cafeteria. Months before we'd installed turf in our courtyards. A torrential rain had come overnight, and the turf didn't allow the rain to drain through as quickly as we'd hoped. The overflow of water came into our building under the hallway doors.

By the time the custodians arrived, the hallways were already under more than 3 inches of water. Students couldn't reach their classrooms without treading through the water. No one knew the extent of the flooding in the rest of the building. In order to determine our next steps, someone would need to walk through the waters to examine the extent of the damage. There was a possibility that there were surge protectors and computer plugs submerged in the water, creating a risk of electrocution. I put my bag down, grabbed a walkie talkie from my office and began walking through it. As I reached each hallway, I radioed back to let them know the condition of each wing of the school.

We quickly drafted a plan to have the students come around to the back of the building to enter their classrooms. Paraprofessionals and teachers helped to escort nearly 400 students across the front of the campus. We limited movement for the remainder of the morning until our operations team removed the excess water with wet vacuums. The regional superintendent even came out in his suit to help push the water out of the building on that morning. We even had a parent come in to assist with mopping up a few remaining wet spots in the hallways. Lunches for our students were delivered to classrooms on rolling carts that afternoon. That moment of being the one to take the step into the depths of uncertainty is what the principalship is all about. When a crisis happens, you need a team that can help you to quickly develop a plan of action and then execute the plan. Sometimes you have to step in a salty situation in your best suede shoes and just start walking. It was during that experience that the title of this book first came to mind: Principals Don't Walk on Water – They Walk Through It.

The waters of educational leadership have become even more brackish in recent months due to the Trump administration's inability to communicate a clear plan for the reopening of schools. During the first two months of school closings, the Secretary of Education was noticeably absent from the podium in the midst of the most significant disruption to public education this century. Either she refused to stand in those brackish waters, or she was given a directive to remain silent. Our schools and communities deserve leaders that are willing to own the moment and take control when we need them most.

President Trump has a severe aversion to brackish waters. When the White House press corps asks tough questions, he fires back with off the cuff responses that are irresponsible and rude. His responses are less than presidential. He fails to follow the guidance of his own public health 'experts' and consistently contradicts their recommendations with his own. What we are witnessing is the antithesis of real leadership. He finds himself floundering in the brackish waters of leadership when he is best suited for the set of reality television where scripts and editing can limit what we see. I think we've all seen enough.

Teachers and families deserve to know what a return to school will look like this fall. Many districts have rolled out plans that offer parents options for virtual learning or blended models. The health and mental wellness of my staff is a priority for me. We have many members of the profession who possess high risk factors that would make exposure to Covid-19 catastrophic. We must not put them in harm's way until there is a clear plan in place to protect the members of our profession. This includes additional training for staff on maintaining a contaminant-free environment, protocols for parents who want to visit classrooms, and safety measures for the buses that bring hundreds of students to our schools.

I've been thoroughly impressed with the response of Mayor Ras Baraka during this crisis. His courage to stand and deliver updates the citizens of Newark is a blueprint for how school leaders should enter this space in 2020. There is a consistent flow of information and people need to be kept in the know as things change. As Mayor Baraka approaches the podium during his weekly press conferences, he is always in a mask, modeling the recommendations he pushes out to his community. He engages his constituents, answering their question directly from the live chat. He demonstrates the ability to sustain a high level of professionalism in waters that could potentially become brackish at any moment. He does this with the poise and class that is befitting of a true leader. In fact, Mayor Baraka was once a principal of a high school in Newark prior to his foray in the world of politics.

It is healthy for a leader to have a change of mind given additional information about a matter. The premise for my book, "The Mountain Principles," is that school leaders and business leaders are constantly learning and growing through our struggles and challenges. The leaders' position on any issue can't be so rigid that it becomes unchangeable; but he can't be so easily swayed that any complaint or concern causes him to waver and waft from his stance like a leaf in a stream.

A leader's position on an important issue should be like lava...solid, but changeable under certain conditions. Like molten lava, moving slowly and deliberately through and around obstacles, the leader's position should be solid enough to maintain its form yet malleable enough to reshape itself when the temperatures reach a certain intensity. Once things cool down, it solidifies. Jim Collins talks about how leaders in organizations respond when things don't go as planned in his book "From Good to Great". Market changes and the need to be competitive force us to rethink our decisions. It's not the we are second guessing ourselves. We are actively assessing the team and determining if people or processes need to be repositioned or revisited. In describing Level 5 leadership he writes, "When things go wrong, we conduct "autopsies without blame"—we seek to understand underlying root causes, rather than pin the blame on an individual. People in our culture are never penalized for bringing forth the brutal facts."

I found much of my time during my first year as a principal consumed with the operational and business side of the house. We were heavily focused on creating an environment conducive to learning, securing the resources for learning, having the discussions to set the stage for learning, and tracking the data related to learning. This summer I decided to make a conscious and concerted effort to shift my focus to spend 80-90% of my time on all things instruction related. That includes observing teachers, offering feedback, conducting walkthroughs to analyze rigor, or finding and sharing resources about best practices. I had to have the courage to take an honest look at how my time was spent last year and make decisions to change my approach.

This year is the year of transformation for us. We are reaping the benefits of our hard work and a deliberate shift from last year as sets of data rolls in. More than the numbers though, the feel of our building is noticeably different as we are collectively bound to a higher purpose related to expectations and social justice. We realize we are setting a trajectory for our students and their families. We understand the social context of our school and the challenges in our community. We, like any team of professionals, find ourselves at moments when adjustments must be made. When it comes to educational leadership, there are moments when the leader has to step in, roll up his or her sleeves, and fix something that's not working. The organization is an organic entity that has many moving parts. What might be perceived as small adjustments have ripple effects on team dynamics, parent relationships, bonds with students, and teachers working within their comfort zones. There are so many puzzling pieces associated with fine tuning a process, staffing, or a long-held school procedure. Sometimes, it's not that anything is broken at all. There may be the possibility of a much more positive outcome if a change is made. Some teachers have a knack for leading small groups, others have mastered the interactions with parents and the "art of diplomacy." Others are instructional technology gurus who help grow every teacher on their team. When the strengths are glaring and the stakes are high, a decision has to be made about a potential change. The question is, does the leader have the courage to make the call?

Implementing restorative practices school-wide seems to be taking a bit longer to become pervasive. The shift toward restorative practices in response to student misbehavior is a mind-shift that some educators embrace fully while others are openly resistant to it. Making sure my staff is knowledgeable about restorative practices helps us bridge the gap between initiation and implementation. The legacy of punishment runs deep in schools. Recently, in my hometown of Augusta, a charter school has decided to bring back paddling as a consequence. I wanted to create an environment where the heavy lifting done by my teachers was in the form of morning meetings and teaching appropriate behaviors. We shifted our principal/student chats toward helping students reflect on incidents and grappling with their impact on school or class culture. It's easy to change policies on paper but mindsets don't change as quickly. Helping teachers, parents and students make the cognitive leap is a process and cultural shift. From the outside looking in, it may be perceived as a more lenient approach to discipline. In actuality, higher numbers of suspensions negatively impact student achievement and ultimately create self-fulfilling prophecies that we are working to change. Teachers have to have the courage to take on a new approach that is less punitive and more grounded in social justice and redemption than punishment and documentation. The leader's job is to make the case, much like a defense attorney, for why a social justice orientation when handling classroom management is a research-based practice that produces better outcomes for our scholars. One of my former principals would advise me to "water the green grass". What she was telling me was to point out and celebrate those teachers and teacher leaders who were successfully implementing school-wide initiatives. Instead of putting all of the energy in places where things weren't growing, we shifted the focus to cultivate and spread the work of some amazing educators. This helped things take root and grow within our school. That same work of 'growing the green grass' is happening at Marbut Traditional Theme School. The leader's job is to make the case, much like a defense attorney, for why a social justice orientation is a research-based practice that produces better outcomes for our scholars.

In the book "How the Way We Talk Can Change the Way We Work", Robert Kegan and Lisa Lahey describe the language of ongoing regard. They suggest that as leaders we have a responsibility to embed structures in meetings that promote a language of appreciation in our school. Each meeting should help to promote a collaborative culture where peers can celebrate one another. This should be part of our school's language in the same way that our language about student achievement is framed in terms of specific data points. During the second year of my principalship, we introduced the P.E.A.K. Performance Awards. P.E.A.K. stands for persistence, effort, achievement, and knowledge. It was a way to identify those peak performers, boost morale, and provide us with insights on what we can all do to be more effective and productive in our roles. The feeling of being inspired by the people you lead is magical. The notion of Employee of the Month never sat well with me. In large schools, there are so many people behind the scenes leading to the success of the team that it seems illogical...somewhat disrespectful, to identify just one person on a team who stands out for the entire month. I want to lift up as many of my team members as I can when I see them going above and beyond. It's one of my obsessions. Whether it is the new custodian who takes great care and pride in his work, or the teacher whose innovative approach to teaching a poetry lesson brings it alive with the theme music from The Fresh Prince of Bel Air.

The lens of the leader can't be so focused on seeing changes in others that we negate the need for making changes in our own belief systems. The greatest transformational leader amongst us is the leader who first has the courage to change himself. Finding ways to broaden the stage and create a warm wave of appreciation that moves through our school has been one of my ongoing professional goals.

It's 2:45 and the weekly staff meeting is about to begin. Teachers slowly waft into the room as slowly as morning fog, hands filled with papers and laptops. They melt into their seats like beads of sweat streaming down an athlete's face. It's a team that has been on the field for 8 hours and now gathers for an hour-long huddle. If exhaustion had a face, this is what it would look like. The chatter of small talk and greetings gradually fades as the principal steps forward and says, "Alright everyone, let's get started..."

For a few years I've been experimenting with a concept of conducting occasional virtual meetings for my staff. After a long day in the classroom, teachers absolutely deserve peaceful moments to plan, grade papers, and begin the transition to family life. Having work-life balance is important for maintaining your sanity in public education.

Nevertheless, there is an abundance of information to share and adjustments to be made that meetings are in inevitable part of the work of educators. State departments of education have been doing webinars for years allowing attendees to tune in to live or pre-recorded presentations about state-wide changes or initiatives. The benefits of virtual meetings include a digital record of information covered and the assurance that everyone hears the same information and can readily execute the same mission. Now schools are thrust into virtual meetings as the norm because of school closures. While I am glad that public education has made this fundamental leap in the use of available technology, I feel that once again we have moved out of necessity rather than the pursuit of ongoing innovation. Public education must keep reflecting on practices and determine how to move forward by choice and not due to the hot-button issue of the moment. This includes reexamining how we register students, communicate with parents, and provide specialized professional development for our staff in formats that fit their schedules.

The Meeting After the Meeting

MRS. PENNIN WAS IN HER SECOND YEAR AS PRINCIPAL of our small neighborhood school in Augusta, GA. She was a middle-aged black woman with salt and pepper hair. She possessed a good sense of how schools should be run and had a stellar reputation as a classroom teacher. She found herself in a familiar space as an early career principal...trying to add her own style to a school community that had been led by the same type of leadership for years. Changing teacher practices takes time. For those of us who were relatively new in our teaching careers, change wasn't as difficult. For many of the veterans though, uploading, downloading, logging in, and disaggregating sounded like a foreign language. During my time as a classroom teacher I can remember how it only took that one teacher at the table to set the tone for how the principal's messages were received. Marquette University conducted research on communication and found that 70% of our communication is nonverbal. It was like watching a daytime drama unfold. As the principal was up front pouring out a month's worth of information, facial expressions, subtle gestures, and rolling eyes deliver their own distinct response to the speaker's message and other attendees. This is one of the very reasons I've never been a fan of long drawn out meetings. The real action and traction happens in the meeting after the meeting when teachers who have been complaining about having to stay for a meeting gather around a car for an additional 35 minutes to discuss the highs and lows of what happened in the meeting and what they planned to do about it. It has been described by leadership theorists as false harmony, leaving a leader thinking that issues have been resolved and that everyone is on the same page. So the emergence of virtual faculty meetings at our school stemmed from my love of technology and my aversion to the idea of too many "staff meetings".

Let's Stay Together

We need face to face meetings but, in my opinion, having them weekly is overkill. When it comes to meetings, the energy of the room is literally dependent on the type of day the school has had. The most skilled presenters have the ability to change the energy in the room with music, activities, or their own stage presence. At our school, when teachers walk into the media center, they might be greeted by a chef serving a meal, the sounds of Buju Banton's Walk Like a Champion or Al Green's Let's Stay Together. We then open up the meeting with wave of celebrations from peers to set the tone. Giving team members a few minutes to fellowship and greet one another is another way to set a positive tone before the start of in-person meetings. What you celebrate in your school becomes an indelible part of your school's culture. If there is silence, be ready to fill it with celebrations of your own. Let them see that you notice what they are doing and will praise them in the presence of their peers. The tone of the meeting is primed by the things that happen at the start of the meeting.

Personalization

In developing my virtual meetings there are a few things I do to personalize the presentation. I keep a notebook with the pressing reminders that need to be shared with all staff. This year I've introduced my leadership team to the Full Focus Journal by Michael Hyatt. I find that it helps us synchronize our way of working, prioritizing and planning. The planner contains sections for us to set yearly goals, quarterly goals, preview the week ahead, and list the top priorities of the day ahead. For those of us accustomed to using a regular agenda calendar type planner, the Full Focus Planner is a way of stretching yourself to be much more intentional about what you plan to do and maximizing every moment of workweek. The contents of the meetings shouldn't be an exhaustive list of upcoming due dates. It should include some humor, references to school culture, as well as some data to underscore the "why" behind important initiatives. I write down the celebrations that need to be brought before them. Several photos from around the school are included to give the presentation less of a 'template' feel. These are typically photos of our staff in collaborative planning, students in class working, and teachers actively delivering instruction. I use these images as the background of the presentation. The staff never knows when their photo or lesson will be the featured image on a slide so in it adds a layer of recognition and surprise to the presentation.

Absenteeism, Distortion & Amnesia

When people miss the meeting because of an appointment or an absence, they inevitably ask the most unreliable sources for the high points. "What did I miss?" A well-intentioned colleague casually replies, "Oh, nothing, we just went over some stuff about rigor and standards." Now, the impact that you hoped to see from your well-planned meeting has just gone out the window for the teachers who were not there. Then there's the ways people distort a leader's commentary to fit their own more tantalizing narrative of school scandal and controversy. I can remember speaking to my staff about a rodent issue that we needed to address. I emphasized keeping our classrooms clean and floors free of debris. I told them that this was not meant to alarm students and parents, but we needed to be more proactive about keeping our facility rodent and pest free. As one of my staff members loves to say, my words were very quickly "sliced and diced, scattered, smothered and covered" in a way that made it seem like there was a Watergate level cover-up at our school. Within days, news media was parked outside, there were social media posts, questions from parents. All of this from words being taken out of context in a meeting.

Sometimes the issue isn't absenteeism nor distortion but a form of academic selective amnesia. Having a digital record of expectations helps to heal this disorder that can be pervasive in its absence. Standards posted? Lesson plans printed? Who knew? Thankfully, these bouts of academic dementia aren't widespread, but they do emerge every so often.

The Formula

My team can always expect to receive a meeting agenda in advance of the meeting. There are no surprises about what is going to be covered. For the virtual meetings, there are always certain components: an after-meeting action, a confirmation of viewing, and a brief assessment of the content. I use Canva.com to create the presentations. I then download them into a PowerPoint format and add the voiceovers to each slide. Once I've gone through the entire presentation, I share it with the team and establish a timeline for viewing. Using Microsoft Forms as the platform for the after-meeting quiz allows me to monitor who has viewed the meeting, how many minutes it takes to complete the task, and their responses to the questions from the meeting.

The expectations for teachers to administer assessments, collect data, analyze data, plan instruction, and differentiate has made limited time an even more precious commodity. They need time to plan, to copy, to think and time to meet with their teammates. Grade level meetings and collaborative planning are place where master teachers are forged. Rich discussions about what's working, what's not working and healthy debates about best practices give me life. These are the meetings I love to join in on...small grade level meetings where we discuss their innovations, assessment data, and next steps to ensure mastery. These small, intimate and productive meetings are a much better use of time than the large staff meetings that are not as specialized in their content. Adding the virtual meeting into the repertoire of innovative practices makes sense in this era of Facetime, video-conferencing, and online coursework. The best leaders learn to spend part of the month with their heads in clouds. The investment in the virtual meeting is an investment in teacher morale and clarity of messaging.

Recommendations

Any leader would do well to broaden your radar to begin studying the leadership you see around the country and pull from it to add to your own tool kit. There are so many parallels to be found in the business world, politics, and the military. Education has a different culture, but the approaches to leadership from other professions can be easily adapted to the work we do on a daily basis. We partnered with a nationally known non-profit called The New Teacher Project (TNTP) in 2019 and convened several focus groups. Their work in education reform is documented in studies they've done on the opportunity myth which suggests that many students are not actually exposed to grade level standards for much of the school day. Teachers and leaders have to be especially mindful of not perpetuating the myth that if students are kept engaged in 'work' that we are assuring parents that their scholars are ready for the next grade level. Our partnership with TNTP brought light to the disparity between the high number of awards we were passing out and the low levels of academic growth we were seeing from one grade to another. In my first meeting of the year, we looked at the data and the room became silent. During the transition to virtual learning in Spring of 2020, that partnership became a key ingredient in helping my teachers make the leap into virtual classrooms to support student learning until the end of the year.

One focus group we convened during our work with TNTP prior to the school closures consisted of parents from various backgrounds. The parents gave us critical feedback on what they valued in our school. They also expressed their concerns about the school, our communication, leadership, and overall instructional program. Next, we convened a student focus group.

This group of scholars from all grade levels shared with us how they felt about our school. They talked about the quality of the lunches, the celebrations, morning announcements, and the school uniform. Giving these two groups a more salient voice in the school became a top priority of my principalship. People will ultimately respect your transparency and appreciate your honesty.

My advice to aspiring principals would be this: while working to preserve a sense of democracy within the school, know that you have to ultimately make calls that may not win popular opinion. In those instances, over communicate the rationale, helping the team to see all sides of the issue and why a certain decision was made. People will ultimately respect your transparency and appreciate your honesty. At the end of the day, be able to sit in your office chair, close your eyes, and feel content with the choices you made to move your school forward.

The nation has been in turmoil over the decision of whether to reopen schools in light of the spike in cases of Covid-19. School boards and superintendents around the nation are having to weigh the touch decisions of protecting the safety of the community, postponing the start of school, and determining next steps for instructional delivery. The cancellation of graduations has been a hot button point because it marks a milestone for the Class of 2020 that many people feel should not be taken away from them. This specific moment exemplifies the types of tough decisions that principals have to make on a daily basis. We go into this work with the clear understanding that these are brackish waters. We accept that everyone we serve will not appreciate our service. We accept and commit to the challenge.

Chapter 3: We Don't Love These Holes

*"But when the assembly gathered in opposition to Moses
and Aaron and turned toward the tent of meeting,
suddenly the cloud covered it and the glory of
the Lord appeared."*

Numbers 16:14

W E'D JUST ENDED OUR TITLE I ANNUAL MEETING
AND AS THE PARENTS BEGAN FILING OUT OF
THE CAFETERIA, I SAW ONE PARENT
APPROACHING ME AND SMILING. I knew her
well from afternoon dismissal. Her daughter
was one of our best 5th grade students and
I'd recently remarked to her mother that her daughter's report
card grades and MAP scores were impressive. Both of them
beamed with pride and a bit of surprise at knowing that the
principal was checking up on her progress and performance. On
this evening though, she had something she wanted to share with

me. She started by saying, "Thank you for tonight. Now I understand the numbers and how things are calculated. I have to tell you that when you first came here, I had to get used to all of the changes. But now, after three years, I can see what you are doing. I can see you are in it for the right reasons. You are all about the kids." I smiled and thanked her for the support and honesty.

Then, with a bit of hesitation, she continued as a look of concern replaced her smile, "You know, I have to tell you, some of your own teachers were really working against you last year too. But most of them have moved on. Keep doing what you are doing. We see the difference you are making."

The Sailboat Theory

Imagine that the school is a large sailboat traveling through choppy waters. Nearly all of the crew is on the deck shifting sails and holding on, trying to help the captain steer the ship through treacherous waters. We realize that we are in the throes of the storm and we will either survive together or sink to the depths of the foamy waters around us. Missing from this picture are a few members of the team who should be on deck helping. Instead, they are on the lower deck actively drilling holes in the ship to hasten our descent. Somehow, they fail to understand that they are working to sink the very vessel they are aboard.

Leaders in any industry have to accept the fact that there will be members of the team who have not bought into the vision or the mission of the organization. Sometimes it's an ideological clash or personality conflict. Leadership styles vary, and as organizations change the priorities shift and the expectations for performance increase. This can create tension and factions begin to form throughout organizations, schools, or churches. Efforts to undermine the work can become as extreme as folks researching and disseminating your driving history in an effort to create distractions from the tasks at hand. Embracing and overcoming the resistance requires a thick skin, inner fortitude, and a healthy sense of humor.

The PowerPoint Principle

Scraping the surface to determine why folks actively work to drill holes in their own ship can lead to a number of conclusions. Many educators are married to old methods and practices that have become second nature to them. Pushing folks beyond their comfort zone can evoke resistance. One recent example of this is what I call "The PowerPoint Principle". PowerPoint was developed nearly 40 years ago. I enter classrooms where students are engaged in research and still learning on this program that was once a cutting-edge technology. I would encourage any educator to introduce their students to the ten PowerPoint alternatives for 2019. The PowerPoint Principle is this: Never allow your skills to become outdated. You can't build for the future with antique tools. Information is power and teachers have to remain current in order to keep up.

The Harvard Business Review published an article entitled "Choosing Strategies for Change" in 2013 The article outlines the 3 steps for managing change successfully:

1. Analyze the situational factors
2. Determine the optimal speed for change
3. Consider methods for managing resistance

The authors, Kotter & Schlesinger (2013), provide leaders with five methods to address "these holes" being drilled into our ships as leaders implementing change. The methods are education, participation, facilitation, negotiation, and coercion. In the middle of my 10th year in educational leadership, I can recall using each of these methods in some way to address resistance.

Education: The solution to stop "these holes" from being drilled may be an honest conversation about why certain initiatives are being implemented. Whether it's from student performance or a parent survey, data tells a story and can be the impetus for a call to action. We decided last year that our uniform policy needed stricter enforcement. We started the year off on the same page. Students and parents had a clear understanding of the expectation. Recently students suggested 'free dress days. I knew this wouldn't go over well with my staff unless it was aligned to a school-wide initiative. I explained that we would only consider a 'free dress day' if it was in support of one of our academic initiatives. We decided that the monies raised would benefit our

Urban Agriculture program. Educating the students on the convergence of our interests was an amenable resolution. Likewise, teachers understood and didn't perceive it as a compromise on our policy but rather as a strategic student-led fundraiser in support of our collective work.

Participation: I was once told that the best leaders "run to their resisters" to participate in school-wide initiatives. Call them up onto the deck, drop the drill for a moment, and come help to lead this project. Let them share their perspective in a way that is tied to the overall mission of the school. In 2013 I worked with a team of 10 high school department chairs in Augusta. I noticed that during our department meetings a few guys were frequently disengaged from the discussion. I devised a plan to have them as part of the agenda of every meeting. One would share a success from his team, another would share a best practice, while another would facilitate a group activity.

Facilitation: We've been implementing Guided Reading school-wide. At times, what is perceived as resistance is linked to a knowledge gap. They may just not know how to do it effectively yet. Creating a culture where a growth mindset is conveyed by the leadership is key. "We're not there yet, but just wait!" Facilitating peer observations and ongoing professional development can absolve the anxiety and resistance to a non-negotiable expectation.

I once hired a teacher who came into the classroom with a wealth of experience and Power Point presentations aligned to the 5th grade math standards. He could have stuck to those

Power Points for years. Instead, when I introduced him to Canva, a graphic design software that allows you to create dynamic presentations, obtain a shareable link, and make edits to the linked material in real time, he added the app to his repertoire. He became a stronger teacher because of his openness to new ideas. Sometimes people resist a new approach or new technology because they are fearful that they will fail at mastering it. Now our school has an optional course where teachers can learn how to use Canva.

Negotiation: In 2000, I worked for Merrill Lynch in the World Financial Center in lower Manhattan. As the trading volume increased, we were called upon to work overtime to process the high volume of trades that were being bought and sold on the New York Stock Exchange. In addition to receiving overtime pay, they provided dinner and a chauffeur driven ride home if you worked past 9 pm. Negotiating with staff can include providing incentives for peak performance such as comp time, early leave, meals, or special recognition for helping the organization meet its objectives.

Manipulation and co-optation: While Schlesinger and Kotter list manipulation and co-optation as methods for managing change, they note that this approach can undermine the leader's ability to successfully use education or participation.

In transforming school communities, principals violate trust at their peril. Relationships are critical. I avoid manipulation and co-optation.

Coercion: This is the most basic tool for addressing resistance. Helping team members understand that we rise and fall together. The climate of accountability in public education leans in this direction, linking performance and achievement to school ratings, career trajectories and teacher evaluations. Consistent and successful execution of expectations tied explicitly to performance reviews can effectively fill "these holes" being drilled in the ship.

Helping the crew members preoccupied with drilling either find their way up to the main deck to assist in the work or off of the ship is the job of the leader. The ever-present sound of drilling will always be heard in the depths of a ship moving in the right direction. Responding to the sound, implementing appropriate countermeasures, and filling the holes is part of the journey of leadership. Ask any leader about resistance and they will share stories of push back, passivity, and apathy on many fronts. Those of us who lead accept it as part of the journey we love. Schools are organic spaces where things are either growing or becoming stagnant. We love seeing teachers thrive, students learning, and parents actively woven into the fabric of the school community. The work of the leader is a labor of love. Nevertheless, we don't love these holes.

"The job of a revolutionary is, of course, to overthrow unjust systems and replace them with just systems because a revolutionary understands this can only be done by the masses of the people.

-Kwame Ture

Chapter 4: Seeds of Change

He replied, "Because you have so little faith. Truly I tell you, if you have faith as small as a mustard seed, you can say to this mountain, 'Move from here to there,' and it will move. Nothing will be impossible for you."

Matthew 17:20

WHEN SCHOOLS REFINE THEIR FOCUS AND SYNERGIZE ALL THEIR EFFORTS AROUND INNOVATIVE INITIATIVES THEY BEGIN TO, SOMETIMES LITERALLY, SEE THE FRUITS OF THEIR LABOR. This summer, a team of teachers from Marbut Traditional Theme School met to discuss our ongoing school improvement plans. We'd been pursuing STEAM certification for years with no real traction. We needed to be more specific about our focus and determine which aspect of STEAM we'd center our collective work around. Our school is unique in that it operates on a lottery system and students are selected from the attendance zones of four other schools. Many of our students live in "food deserts". The USDA suggests that over 23 million people in the United States reside in food deserts where access to affordable, healthy food options are limited or non-existent. With a sprawling campus spread across 2 acres and a building of over 91,000 square feet, it was decided that our green spaces lent themselves well to a focus on urban agriculture. We already had a butterfly garden, a vegetable garden, and had recently built 3 additional planting boxes in the front of school with support from parents and community sponsors.

My excitement around the ideas of urban agriculture can be traced back to my South Georgia roots. My father majored in Agriculture at Fort Valley State University and he and my mother spent a considerable amount of time gardening and landscaping around our home. Directly behind our house was a vast cornfield. When asked what I wanted to become in 4th grade, I quickly replied "A farmer". My choice was based on a field trip I took with my class where we visited a farm and met with Mr. Alford McKenzie, an African-American farmer. He served as the county extension agent from 1963 to 1986. As he showed us his crops and his cattle, he was planting seeds in my mind that would emerge nearly four decades later.

A Community Effort

During the summer of 2019, our vegetable garden produced a large crop of collard greens, tomatoes, cucumbers and bell peppers. We continued to brainstorm ways to expand the reach of the garden as an outdoor classroom. Our STEAM teacher, Mr. Anthony Mays, began visiting other STEAM certified schools to gather ideas. Upon returning, he would meet with me, share the innovations he observed and redeliver to the faculty to get their insights and reach a consensus about what projects truly aligned to our goals and school culture.

With a refined focus on urban agriculture, we had a much better net for attracting the right types of community partners. One of our first partners in this work was Mr. Ryan Dunn who had worked with other metro-Atlanta schools on setting up aquaponics systems where students could grow vegetables that were nourished by the waste from adjacent fish tanks. It was a way to extend our urban agriculture work beyond the gardens and planting boxes. Most importantly, it broadened our student's exposure to ways that foods are produced. Momentum began to build around this idea of urban farming. Mr. Dunn met with the faculty to discuss how aquaponics provides an opportunity to expose students to the science of food production as well as the economic potential of urban agriculture. He returned to the school later in the week to speak with parents at a PTA meeting. We began to share more information about our focus on urban agriculture in our school newsletter and on our Facebook page. Parents could see what was growing in the garden and what they could do to support our efforts. We received donations of potting soil and plants. A local hardware store donated lumber to build more planting boxes.

Most recently, a staff member reached out to a park ranger who visited the school to assess the campus for planting 10 fruit trees. He determined an ideal location based upon the number of hours of sunlight the trees would need. Installing an orchard of fruit trees would be a lasting investment on the campus that would provide experiences for future students and families for years to come. Our PTA has been especially supportive of this work, adding a line item in the budget in support of STEAM and campus beautification.

We realized that we needed to be intentional about our focus so that it was very clear to a visitor that we are exploring ideas around container gardens, aquaponics, and hydroponics. Fortuitously, our lobby is designed with skylights, creating a space where natural light pours in throughout the entire day. We brought in containers and planted kale, cabbage, basil, and tomatoes. Beyond the lobby, we began to research school-wide growing projects that could be implemented in every classroom with minimal time investment from the teachers. We decided to begin growing sweet potatoes by cutting them in half, partially submerging them in water, and allowing them to take root. Students and teachers can keep data on the growing process and plant them in the garden in the Spring.

The parallels between teaching and farming teach us lessons about ourselves. Urban farming, like teaching, requires a level of resourcefulness. As we have rolled out our school-wide planting projects, you see vast differences in how teachers problem-solve and improvise. One's ability to find alternative solutions, elicit support, or brainstorm with a team on these projects comes across in their teaching and grade level collaborations as well. Those teachers who are dependent on others to solve their problems or use obstacles as excuses to stall implementation carry that approach into every aspect of their lives. One of my mantras is "Champions don't make excuses, they make adjustments." I say this to students over the intercom and to staff members in faculty meetings. Masterful teachers understand that learning is a process of creating the right environment for growth to occur. They understand that certain students grasp concepts quickly and others need a different set of conditions to reach mastery just as certain seeds take longer to germinate than others. With a committed staff and supportive community, we are planting seeds of change.

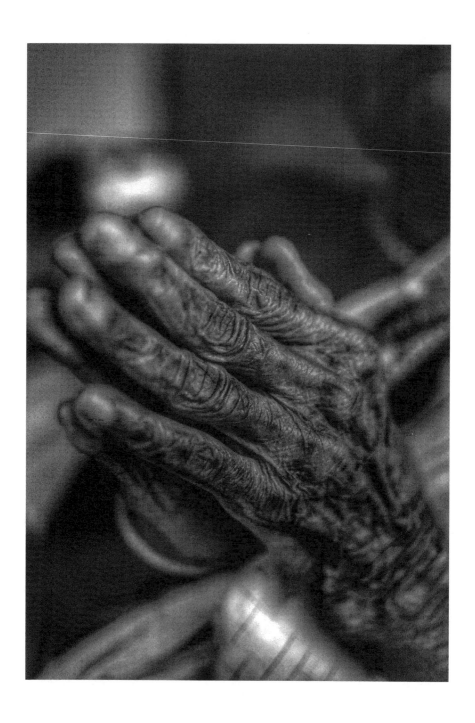

Chapter 5: Principals on the Prayer Line

Righteousness is not that you turn your faces toward the east or the west, but [true] righteousness is [in] one who believes in Allah, the Last Day, the angels, the Book, and the prophets and gives wealth, in spite of love for it, to relatives, orphans, the needy, the traveler, those who ask [for help], and for freeing slaves; [and who] establishes prayer and gives zakah; [those who] fulfill their promise when they promise; and [those who] are patient in poverty and hardship and during battle. Those are the ones who have been true, and it is those who are the righteous.

Surah Al-Baqurah 2:177, The Holy Qu'ran

ANALYTICAL PSYCHOLOGIST CARL JUNG INTRODUCED THE CONCEPT OF 'SYNCHRONICITY' IN THE 1920'S AS THE PRINCIPLE OF "MEANINGFUL COINCIDENCES". Nothing that occurs in our complex lives is an accident. Events that have no causal relationship are meaningfully related. My most recent experience with synchronicity occurred as I joined a conference call with fellow principals in our metro-Atlanta school district.

Our district has been going through a major transition in recent weeks. The superintendent and the district recently severed their ties six months earlier than expected. We met the interim superintendent on the previous week during an administrator meeting. As the Thanksgiving Break looms in near future, principals are scrambling to complete the required observations of teachers by the November 29th deadline. The pressure is mounting on every principal in the district as the time ticks by. Fortunately, our regional superintendent understands the urgency of the time and honors that by arranging a conference call to share some important information in lieu of a meeting.

The conference call had been scheduled for 9:30, giving me enough time to do a few observations before returning to my office to join the call. I checked my phone and dialed the number that had been sent to us via text by the regional superintendent. After a prompt, I entered the access code to join the conference. A recorded voice says, "Please announce yourself". I say, "Andre Mountain, Marbut Elementary". Within seconds, I'm hearing a list of other principals joining the call. I can hear the regional superintendent on the call listing the names of those of us who had already joined and making sure we were all accounted for. In the midst of his roll call and the intermittent tone of others joining the call there was a woman's voice that began to become more salient. *"Father God, we come to you in need of*

---

your blessing and your favor, Father God." Everyone is silent, and the regional superintendent reminds us, "Principals, please mute your phones". Everyone mutes their phones, causing the voice of woman to become noticeably louder. In seconds it becomes clear what we are hearing.

"Father God, we thank you for your grace and mercy. Father God watch over our families, our children, our sick loved ones. Father God, we know you are here with us. Father God bless our children as they move through this community, Father God. These people are out here harming our babies, Father God. We need your guidance Father God. Help us, Father God, guide our steps. We thank you Father God…"

As we are listening, we are all trying to recognize the voice of this mysterious prayer leader. It sounded like an older woman who was an experienced prayer leader. Was one of the principals praying and possibly forgot to mute her phone? I started trying to figure out who it could be…Principal Davis? Principal Goolsby? I texted Mrs. Davis, "I hear a prayer." She texts back, "Me too." By this time, the regional superintendent has stopped talking because the voice of the prayer had become the dominant voice on the call. The automated voice began to announce principals as they left the conference call. I hesitated to leave because I was beginning to connect to the prayer.

Somehow, instead of dialing in to our region's conference call, we'd all dialed in to a prayer line and heard exactly what we needed to hear to launch our work for the day. Fifteen school leaders were on the receiving end of a prayer for our schools,

families and our communities. It was not what we'd planned to
hear, but it was what we all needed at a moment when we are
entering a season where giving thanks is celebrated. It was a
wrong number at the perfect moment when the backdrop of our
work in schools is impacted by the tensions of leadership
transitions, test scores, and violence in our community.
Synchronicity, as Carl Jung describes it, is about finding purpose in
"meaningful coincidences". Professor Roderick Main suggests that
"meaningful coincidences re-connect us to our spiritually alive
surroundings."

After reluctantly leaving the prayer, I noticed that the
regional superintendent sent us a group text message. He wrote,
"Will try to get another group call number. You can end the initial
call." I texted, "Amen." Another principal texted, "Thank you
Father God."

These unpredictable moments have occurred often
throughout my principalship. Just as we would be looking for a
new community partner, a successful former student would walk
through the door and introduce themselves as an alumnus
looking to give back to Marbut. It is amazing how the universe
responds to what we ask, and prayers are answered when we
make a genuine request to our higher power.

As a principal, asking is half the battle. One of my mentors,
Lucille Sharper would often tell me, "You have not because you
ask not." She was reminding me to get out into the community
and let people know what you need. This advice would be
instrumental in our school getting many goals accomplished

successfully over the course of the last three years. When I arrived in 2017, the school only had three very old vacuum cleaners. Most of the 27 classrooms had large carpets where students would congregate for stories each day. We put a call out to our Marbut parents that we were in need of vacuums via a flyer. We specified the brand and model that we needed because of the frequency of use. In one week, we had 4 vacuums high quality vacuum cleaners donated.

On another occasion, we planned a campus beautification day. I was completely overwhelmed by the outpouring of time, plants and talent that parents and students contributed to beautify our campus. They arrived early on a Saturday morning with garden equipment, gloves, plants and potting soil. Earlier that week, I'd visited Lowes and met with the manager who agreed to donate a generous amount of lumber to our school for our upcoming project to build planting boxes. When the day arrived, the parents came through on the commitments they made to assist with the campus beautification day. They built planting boxes in front of the school with lumber donated to the school by Lowes. We filled those boxes with generous amounts of their donated soil and plants that were purchased by our PTA. At the end of the day, we were all extremely tired. As we looked at the campus with its freshly build planters, seedlings planted, and fresh mulch around the shrubbery, we all felt a sense of collective accomplishment.

Chapter 6: Nurture Student Activism

THE WEEK PRECEDING THE THANKSGIVING BREAK IS A BUSY ONE FOR ANY SCHOOL PRINCIPAL. THERE ARE EVALUATIONS TO BE COMPLETED AND PARENT EVENTS THAT REQUIRE ATTENTION. In my movements through Marbut's hallways over the last few weeks I've encountered two fourth grade students who continue to politely remind me that they would like to meet to revisit a proposal they shared with me in October. Our school recently partnered with TNTP (The New Teacher Project) to enhance the ways we access parental engagement and student voice. A student focus group was convened, and students were asked to share ideas about what could be done to improve the school from their perspective. Melissa Jones-Clarke, a TNTP Performance Coach, facilitated the focus group and remarked that the students were "sharp and articulate about what they wanted to accomplish and where they wanted to go in the future".

In early October they arrived at my office door smiling and asking for "just a moment to discuss an important matter". The language was so precise and polished that I welcomed the conversation and settled back in my chair to hear what these two fourth graders had to say. While our school has a strict uniform policy, these two 4th grade students proposed a "free dress day" for students to express their individuality. I shared with them that our school model and tradition includes required uniforms. I explained that we had tried to do "Free Dress Fridays" in the past but it became an issue with behavior.

So here we were, weeks later and I was cornered with another request to meet and follow up on the initial meetings. "Ah, yes...I remember. You wanted to discuss the dress code and possibly having a free dress day, correct?" They beamed with pride and replied, "Yes!" I said, well Mondays are really busy, let's plan to meet tomorrow. Come see me during your Specials time and we can discuss it." Honestly, I assumed they'd soon forget about their plan to upend our strict dress code for a proposed "free dress" day for students. Tuesday arrived and as I was on my way to do an observation I encountered Alina who smiled and politely reminded me, "Excuse me Mr. Mountain, yesterday you said Mondays were very busy, so we were following up to see if we could possibly meet with you today to discuss our proposal about the dress code?" Inside I was conflicted because of my pride in the persistence of these two students to tactfully present a proposal with such professionalism and grace. On the other hand, I was annoyed that they actually remembered and followed up with me in the midst of my busy schedule. More than anything else, I was reminded that we are educating our students to intentionally disrupt the status quo and become citizens who advocate for change in productive and meaningful ways. How could I make this experience more meaningful for them as a community service project with a convergence of interests for the school and the students?

As we strolled into my office, these two 4th graders already had an aura of victory and we hadn't even discussed the proposal. They reminded me that we planned to do one day each month of free dress where the uniform policy would be waived. Recently, I've been reading "Empire State of Mind" by Zack O'Malley Greenburg. The book chronicles the rise of Jay-Z to an industry mogul. One of the points Greenburg makes is Jay-Z's penchant for asking during a business deal, "What's in it for me?" Essentially, he wants to know in any business dealings, how can our interests converge to create positive outcomes for both parties. This is where we found ourselves on this fateful afternoon in my office. We decided that we needed to make the free dress day in support of a school-wide initiative. Our STEAM focus is Urban Agriculture, so we decided to align the "free dress day" with a fundraiser for our Urban Agriculture program. Students would donate $1.00 in support of our STEAM program to support aquaponics, hydroponics and container gardening. We'd be able to purchase plants and seeds for the Spring season.

Recommendation

This experience reminded me as a school leader to always be open to providing a space for students to advocate for change even when it appears to send ripples through our own school community. Education means much more than test results and grades. Seeing students develop a proposal, advocate for others, and show persistence and professionalism is the authentic application of what we teach to students about activism and effecting change. The question is "Are we prepared to hear them when they speak?"

Chapter 7: Trouble the Waters

Barrier: an obstacle that prevents movement or access.

THE STRING OF ISLANDS WE REFER TO AS THE BARRIER ISLANDS ALONG GEORGIA'S COASTLINE PROTECT THE MAINLAND FROM STORM SURGES. THESE ISLANDS HAVE A HISTORY OF THEIR OWN OF BARRIERS, OVERCOME BY THE WILL OF COURAGEOUS INDIVIDUALS WHO SURVIVED ENSLAVEMENT, CHALLENGED DISCRIMINATION, AND RESHAPED THE SOCIAL ORDER.

On the evening of November 28, 1858, the last shipment of slaves to arrive in Georgia from the Congo in West Africa landed along the southern shore of Jekyll Island, Georgia on a ship called "The Wanderer". It was indeed a grotesque conspiracy that included the then owners of Jekyll, John and Henry DuBignon. The Wanderer docked in the West African nation of Angola on October 4, 1858. Angola was dominated by the Portugese. Congress had banned the importation of slaves since 1808. There were 487 slaves taken aboard, but only 409 survived the journey and emerged from the ship on Jekyll's southern shore. The owner of the slave ship, William Corrie partnered with businessman Charles Augustus Lamar to have the slaves shipped from Jekyll to Savannah, Augusta, and parts of South Carolina. This group of slaves were brought to Jekyll to avoid the attention they might have received had they been brought in through the much busier seaport of Savannah. This afternoon I walked along those same shores with the students of Marbut Traditional Theme School.

With ample historical accounts, images, and artifacts that detail this fascinating history, it seems implausible that it would not appear prominently in the current curriculum for Social Studies in Georgia. The historical significance of Jekyll Island for students in Georgia runs deep. Its inclusion into the existing narrative would add a greater degree of regional history, diversity and cultural relevance to a curriculum that provides a cursory examination of the arrival and persistent struggle of people of color in Georgia. Three survivors of the ordeal, Cilucangy, Pucka Geata, and Tahro (pictured here) recall the capture, the stench, and the horror of their enslavement. Their faces tell a story that refuses to be buried by the sands of time.

We took 47 students to what was once known as the historic St. Andrews Beach. Once, the only beach accessible to African-Americans, St. Andrews beach is a little known slice of African-American history nestled along the pristine beaches of Georgia's Jekyll Island. Prior to 1955, there were no beaches in the state of Georgia that permitted African Americans to enjoy the sun and sand with their families. In fact, in the 1940's, three African-American women were jailed for donning swimsuits and attempting to visit the beach on Jekyll. Once opened, St. Andrews beach became an incubator of thriving black businesses including a hotel, restaurants, and a performance hall. We often hear of those heroes who battled segregation in institutions such as schools and sports leagues. We hear little about those individuals who worked to ensure that everyone could have access to the often-overlooked freedoms we enjoy today.

Today, the land that was once called St. Andrews beach is now home to 4-H's Camp Jekyll. In partnership with the University of Georgia, they provide environmental education to students. I first visited the site in 1985 as a 5th grade student, just two years after 4-H first leased the site. Now, some 34 years later, I returned with a group of 5th graders to explore the same beaches with them as we extend their classroom experiences to the shores of Jekyll. Students' dissected sharks, learned about endangered sea turtles, explore the marsh, and took a class on ornithology.

As we boarded the charter bus to head to our canoeing activity, I noticed all of the students rushed to the back of the bus. I asked them all to fill in the seats from the front of the bus. Our driver, Mr. Johnny Houseworth, an African-American man in his 60's, smiled at this and began to tell me that he was in the 4th grade when Dr. King was killed. He stated that it was then that he decided that he'd never again sit in the back of a bus. Before we left to begin canoeing, Mr. Houseworth offered us a grim warning: "Don't y'all fall in dat wawtah!" Small, intimate, teachable moments continued to occur throughout the trip that will likely leave a lasting impression on these metro-Atlanta students.

Recommendation

One of the highlights of our trip included a very candid conversation with our students about the legacy of struggle of people of color and how they are an extension of that struggle. After dinner, under a pavilion near what was once called the Negro Beach House, we spoke to them about the significance of this place and their choices. The impact of this trip was two-fold as we shared with students the cultural relevance of St. Andrews beach and they gained an environmental education throughout the experience. At once we are asking our students to look back at their legacy, look ahead toward their future, and look within at their own potential. The call to action for educators is to gain a deeper knowledge of our history, integrate that knowledge into our conversations with young people, and never allow that history to be forgotten, even if that means we must 'trouble the waters'.

Chapter 8: Leading Where We Dwell

We have different gifts, according to the grace given to each of us. If your gift is prophesying, then prophesy in accordance with your[a] faith; ⁷ if it is serving, then serve; if it is teaching, then teach; ⁸ if it is to encourage, then give encouragement; if it is giving, then give generously; if it is to lead,[b] do it diligently; if it is to show mercy, do it cheerfully.

Romans 12: 6-8

LIVE IN EAST ATLANTA IN THE MIDST OF RESIDENTIAL AND INDUSTRIAL OUTCROPPINGS SHROUDED IN PINE AND OAK. AT 7:45AM, THE STREETS OF LITHONIA ARE SPARSE. IT WAS ONCE NOTED AS ONE OF THE NATION'S WEALTHIEST AFRICAN-AMERICAN ENCLAVES. As the sun rises gently over the Georgia pines, there are a few retirees out walking with their dogs and the occasional jogger putting in their morning miles. On this June morning I was on my way to Marbut Traditional Theme School to meet with my operations team to discuss the progress they are making on preparing our building for students in the Fall. As I turned onto Marbut Road, I noticed someone walking who looked familiar. She was wearing a hijab, so I only caught a glimpse of her face. Looking back in my rearview I could see that it was one of my scholar's parents, carrying what appeared to be a heavy bag and walking in the direction of the school. I drove past, then quickly circled back and asked if everything was okay. She replied in a thick accent, "Hi Mr. Principal. I'm going to the bus stop. I'm on my way to work". Knowing that the bus stop was two miles away, I insisted that she get in so that I could take her there. When she got in, I noticed her face was covered with sweat. I was glad to be of assistance to her, thinking of how God places us in certain positions to do good for others. I've been on the receiving end of these good deeds on many days, so returning the favor was an absolute obligation. On the way to her bus stop she shared with me how the kids were doing. She asked me about my family. She told me that she has an additional scholar coming to our school this Fall. In those few moments we talked about school uniforms, jobs, and the new realities of school openings in 2020. As she exited, I wished her a great day at work and she said, "God bless you Principal Mountain." As I drove back to the school, I thought about the beauty of leading where we dwell. To see our parents in the everyday struggle humbles one to understand that we are here to serve. We serve their scholars and in a broader sense, their families in helping to forge greater access to opportunities and support.

I thought about the educators who lived in my neighborhood as I was growing up in Swainsboro, GA. Mr. Timms, the band director, lived around the corner. Mr. Bright, the bus driver, lived a few blocks away. Mrs. Trice, my Kindergarten teacher, lived just 2 miles away. Their homes were landmarks we'd drive by on our way to other destinations, and I'd hope to get a glimpse of them as we drove past. There is beauty in dwelling where you teach or lead. It embeds you in the energy of the community your students emerge from. You see them in the corner store, grocery stores, and on the sidewalks.

Mr. Solomon is one of my favorite Marbut parents. He works as a cashier at my neighborhood convenience store. His face lights up whenever my daughter and I walk into the store. He greets us in a thick Ethiopian accent, "Doctor! Selam! How are you?" His daughter and my daughter became fast friends during their time at our school. When we visit his store, he insists on having her pick out a treat free of charge. She is always happy to oblige his generosity. He occasionally asks me what he needs to do to help his middle school or high school scholar and I always try to point him in the right direction with a name or a phone number to call. There are days when he refuses to accept payment for my purchase. It's a welcome battle that I gladly lose occasionally. It's all love. It's the beauty of leading where one dwells.

During my time teaching at Monte Sano Elementary in Augusta, GA in the early 2000's, I actually lived across the street from the school. The Summerville neighborhood of Augusta had a quaint southern feel, with historic homes and cottages dating back to the 1920's and 1930's. When our daughter was born, I was able to go home at lunch to check on my wife and our newborn infant, then walk back across the street to pick up my students from lunch. In the evenings while walking the family dog or sitting on our front porch, I'd have conversations with my neighbors about our school and inform them of the great things happening at the school. To this day, I still keep in touch with neighbors Fred and Sallie who were consistent and staunch supporters of Monte Sano Elementary through the years. As principals and teachers had come and gone, they watched from a distance. They loved the neighborhood and the school that served the neighborhood. They watched our daughter grow up and gifted her with a hand-quilted blanket when she was born. They reminded me of the unique personalities that neighborhoods possess and how school leaders must tap into the richness of a community to extend the reach of the school.

How did I end up living in the community of the school I'm leading in 2020? Prior to moving to Atlanta from Washington State, I'd heard about the notorious Atlanta traffic. I dreaded being late to work as a building leader, early in my career. What type of example would I set if I had the misfortune of being consistently late to work due to traffic on I-20 or I-285? I decided to find a place to dwell in the community where I'd be leading that would not require me to have to access any major thoroughfares. Thankfully, we found a place only 4-minutes' drive from the school. I can walk to the school in under 15 minutes. But it's deeper than proximity. It's more about community. I'm better connected to the community I serve by living in the midst of it. I'm better equipped to understand the challenges they face, the resources at our disposal, and the potential partners and allies we have.

So, this afternoon I noticed that dark clouds were heading in our direction. I began wrapping up my tasks in the office around 6pm, preparing to head home. Set the school alarm, loaded up my car, and pulled out of the school's driveway. As the rain began falling, I noticed a familiar figure walking down the street. It was the same parent I'd dropped off earlier this morning at the bus stop. She was making the 2.5 mile trek back home from the bus stop after a long day of work. I blew my horn, and without a word she came over smiling. Perfect timing and a perfect end to a long day for both of us. She shared that she was from Belize, Central America and the many struggles of finding good schools for her children. In times like these, we need to take better care of one other. Too often the allure and comfort of leadership insulates us from the real-life struggles our families face. Leading is service and service starts in the places where we dwell.

Recommendations

If you can, live near the community where your scholars live. Not only will you save on your commute, but you will have a better connection with their families. We say that it takes a village to raise a child, but over time the village has become increasingly dispersed across large metropolitan areas. If living near your scholars is not possible, then make it a point to do some business in the area so that you can become more familiar with the community they call home. Another way to help bridge the gap between leadership and communities is learning about the small businesses parents operate. Providing them a platform to discuss entrepreneurship with students or to be vendors at school events is a way to support them beyond the classroom.

Harriet Tubman
"the Moses of her People,"
Herself a fugitive, she abducted more
than 300 slaves, leading them
generally through Delaware to
Wilmington and Philadelphia.

Chapter 9: My Heroes Wore Masks

We sing, but oh the clay is vile
Beneath our feet, and long the mile;
But let the world dream otherwise,
We wear the mask!

Paul Laurence Dunbar, "We Wear the Mask"

PAUL LAURENCE DUNBAR WAS ONLY 24 YEARS OLD WHEN HE PUBLISHED THE POEM "WE WEAR THE MASK" IN 1896. It was an honest portrayal of what he saw as the son of freed slaves from Kentucky. Dunbar pulled from the experiences his parents shared about plantation life, coupled with what he witnessed for himself to create poems that hold a mirror up to America. Dunbar self-published his first books while working as an elevator operator and sold them to people for a dollar. He embodied two traits I have tried to integrate into my life as a writer, an entrepreneurial fortitude and the courage to peel back the uncomfortable layers of life in America for the descendants of enslaved Africans.

In many ways, we are beautifully unmasked in 2020 as we reconnect with our heritage in all aspects of our lives. Just yesterday, I spent part of the afternoon making "Hoppin' John", a traditional dish from the South Carolina low country. In a time when the nation is taking issue with "Karens", I stumbled upon a book by Karen Hess, The Carolina Rice Kitchen: The African Connection", making a direct link between my dish and the African Diaspora. She writes, *"That technique of cooking rice and beans together was African in origin, and it spread to every part of the Americas that had a significant African presence. Each location developed its own distinctive rice and bean dishes— the Moros y Cristianos of Cuba (made with black beans), the Pois et Riz Collé of Louisiana (made with red beans), and the Hoppin' John of the South Carolina Lowcountry."* Food and agriculture were inherently linked to our collective survival. This is one of the reasons urban agriculture is experiencing a resurgence in urban communities and at schools like the one I lead in metro-Atlanta. Our food was central to our sense of community and tradition. So were masks.

Africans have always used masks for survival. In West African cultures, the mask was not exclusively decorative or ornamental. Masks were used in ceremonies, celebrations of life and death, declarations of war, and to conjure up the spirits of ancestors in times of peril. The masks Dunbar alludes to, the masks forced upon African-Americans in the 1890's are less ceremonial, and more institutional. The metaphor of the mask is perfect yet troubling in its duplicity. While it protects us it can stifle us from breathing freely. It muffles our cries, hides our tears, and disguises our despair. To be considered free and not yet fully free is to wear the mask. To grapple with the fear of speaking out about blatant injustices for fear of the impact on our professional lives is to wear the mask. To see others targeted, murdered, imprisoned, and disenfranchised, and to be forced under threats of violence to remain silent is to wear the mask. Today is a new era in our history where we feel compelled to wear literal masks, but we've grown tired of wearing the masks that have permitted our subjugation and oppression.

Economic Roots

While most of us are living through experiences in America that we have never experienced before, the events are in fact not unprecedented. The context of Dunbar's poem was a time when America was experiencing an economic depression. Wealthy Americans were fearful the uprising and protests they were witnessing would come to their doorsteps. In 1894, Jacob Coxey from Dayton, Ohio formed an "Industry Army" to protest the government's inaction. He and his "army" marched to Washington. Coxey was jailed after he attempted to deliver a speech on the steps of the Capitol.

Dunbar published "Lyrics of Lowly Life" in 1896. It was his first volume of published work. The context of the time paints a clear picture of why this poem, "We Wear the Mask" was included in the volume. There were one hundred and thirteen African-Americans lynched in 1895. Today we are beginning to see a resurgence in reports of lynchings of African-Americans around the country. There was conflict within the African-American community regarding the way forward. Booker T. Washington visited Atlanta in 1895 and delivered the Atlanta Compromise where he espoused accommodation to White rule and an assurance of basic education and judicial due process. Frederick Douglass had died on February 20th of the same year. W.E.B. DuBois disagreed with Booker T. Washington and felt African-Americans should engage in civil rights activism. This stance would eventually lead to the Civil Rights movement which emerged in the 1950's. Today we see opposing sides regarding the issue of protests, Black Lives Matter, and ways to exert economic pressure on an oppressive criminal justice system.

Most people don't realize that Harriet Tubman was not her real name. Born Araminta Ross, she would become one of the most powerful examples of courage in leadership in American history. Harriet Tubman, born Araminta Ross, conducted at least thirteen missions to rescue families and friends from slavery. She accomplished this with the use of disguises, strategy, and a keen understanding of the deplorable system of oppression she was working to unravel. I would challenge any educator to view your work like the work of Harriet Tubman: working within a system, wearing masks and employing strategies to lead people towards freedom.

Harriet Tubman was the first woman to lead an assault during the Civil War on plantations in South Carolina. In the Combahee River Raid of 1863, she helped 750 slaves to escape plantations and make their way toward Beaufort, South Carolina on Union steamboats. Her mask of invisibility as an African-American woman during the Civil War allowed her to survive as she provided critical information and support to the Union.

At its most critical hour, America is without mature leadership at the highest levels. Our president adds fuel to an increasingly tense political environment by using racist terms and failing to blatantly denounce police misconduct. Instead, we find examples of great leadership in the mayors of our cities like Keisha Lance Bottoms of Atlanta, Ras Baraka of Newark and Mario Cuomo of New York. Mayor Baraka, shown above, distributes masks to Newark's citizens, all the while wearing the mask and gloves recommended by healthcare professionals. The painful juxtaposition of the masked and the unmasked is glaring. As Trump stands at the podium alongside medical experts, some attack him for the fact that he is seemingly unmasked. But I'd suggest that he too IS in fact wearing a mask. He is the host of the grandest masquerade ball and his gilded mask only covers his eyes, preventing him from seeing what is taking place around him. The masks of 1895 have been replaced with N95 masks. The masks we are asked to wear are tangible reminders of the masks my heroes were once forced to wear. Stifling, restrictive, invisible masks.

Recommendations

Develop a deep understanding of the historical oppression of African-American people in the Americas. This is especially key for those working in traditionally underserved and oppressed communities. Context-based pedagogical and leadership approaches enable those who are most often excluded from the curriculum to have a 'seat at the table'. Look around and take long, hard look at the families you are serving. Valuing who they are means learning about them and teaching them what does not appear in the standards.

I would encourage all school leaders to push your teachers go deeper into the curriculum and uncover the uncomfortable truths that exist them. What does this look like? In your feedback to teachers, embed rich examples of other readings, videos and resources that will bring the content to life. Help teachers to move beyond the numerical ratings in their feedback and find the real value in your commentary and subsequent discussions with them. That's where the growth happens. For example, while visiting a 4th grade class last year I observed a teacher delivering a lesson on the concept of Manifest Destiny. In simple terms, Manifest Destiny was the belief by Europeans who came to the Americas that they were entitled to conquer all of the lands they found. In discussing the lesson with him, I challenged him with fully unpacking this belief as a true manifestation of White privilege and a mindset of racial superiority by Europeans. I shared the song "Manifest Destiny" by Jamiroquai with him. I suggested that he contrast this song with the lyrics of the poem "Strange Fruit" which was written by Abel Meeropol and adapted into a song in 1939.

Chapter 10: Where There's Smoke

"My Daddy always said, where there's lots of smoke, there's gotta be a little fire."

Lucille Sharper, Retired Principal

A S I WATCHED WHAT IS HAPPENNED IN AMERICA DURING THE SUMMER OF 2020, I CLENCHED MY PEN AND WAITED FOR THE WORDS TO FLOW. I WAITED FOR THE RIGHT WORDS AND EXPERIENCES TO BUBBLE UP FROM INSIDE MY SOUL. I waited for the pangs of ideas to be born and find their way onto the paper. But they have not yet come. The words have not come because over the course of my 45 years of life, I've become numb to that which the world is just opening their eyes to. This numbness is akin to a persistent pain that one never fully gets comfortable with but begins to grapple

with as part of the reality of now. All I can muster is a few
experiences that paint a picture of what it feels like to be under
the billowing smoke of racism in America.

Smokescreens

So the world is finally starting to awaken to the smell of smoke in
our inner cities in 2020. African-American men's eyes have been
burning from the smoke for years. Music groups like Lady
Antebellum and Dixie Chicks are changing their names. Was
there ever a thought about the feelings behind those names
before now? Companies are redesigning products to remove
stereotypical images. Corporations are manufacturing Band-Aids
of different shades. But the Band-Aids only cover the wounds. The
smoke is still present, and the house is still burning. These surface
level adjustments don't change the heart of American
society. We have to have an honest discussion about how

African Americans are treated in this country and I'm tired talking about it. It's everyone else's turn now.

A Leisurely Drive

My father shared a story with me of being asked to travel to a conference with a White colleague in the early 80's in South Georgia. They were both instructors at the local technical college and typically instructors would carpool when heading to the same event. He decided to drive his own vehicle instead. When she inquired why he didn't ride with her to the conference to save expenses, he explained that they would be driving through small Southern towns and if he needed to stop to rest or use the restroom, he didn't want to have any problems. He'd grown up hearing stories of men turning up missing from driving through the wrong town or being on the wrong side of their own town. He explained that he was less interested in saving money, and more interested in saving his life. There is a level of awareness that he developed growing up in the segregated South that is indelibly engrained in our DNA now. It's a 6th sense that may or may not save us from impending danger. She laughed it off and told him that things had changed. I wish she wasn't wrong.

A Barbershop Experience

Around this same time, I was just at the age when children begin to attempt to make sense of what's fair and unfair. We naturally associate good people with good deeds. We attended a local Kingdom Hall of Jehovah's Witnesses. I always wondered why there were no Black faces in the literature that depicted Biblical times. A White member of our congregation had a barbershop that we'd pass each day on our way from town. My mom asked him if he could cut our hair. He told her that we couldn't come to the shop because he would lose customers. I didn't understand it at the time. I saw him worship with us several times during the week and couldn't understand why he would not welcome us into his barbershop. Looking back, I see that there was a social order that he was not prepared to disrupt for fear of losing profits. Our presence and the presence of our black hair on his clippers would force people to go elsewhere.

The White Knights

Recently, my daughter shared with me that at her tennis camp all the groups had to select names for their team activities. One group of White teenagers selected the name "The White Knights". There were only 2 or 3 African-Americans in the camp. Thankfully, the camp counselors made them change the name. On the way home, I spent time explaining to my daughter who the "White Knights" were. I explained that the White Knights is a name associated with the KKK's practice of terrorizing African-Americans throughout America's history. Deep inside I want to believe it was just a harmless coincidence, but the timing of it burns. To have to have these conversations with an 11 year old at a tennis camp burns. The awareness that I want her to possess is the same awareness that all children should have so they understand how terms and history cast a shadow on the present.

Man's Best Friend

While working as a teacher in Augusta, I crossed paths with Mr. Errin. He was a fellow teacher who shared memories of growing up in South Carolina in the 40's and 50's. He talked about the experience of going to a white family's home to do some yard work. When it was time for dinner, they asked him if he wanted any. He said yes. They brought his dinner out on the porch but allowed the family dog to come in the house and sit with the family as they had dinner. He shared how hurt he felt that he couldn't eat inside with them. I couldn't get the image out of my head of him sitting on that porch eating and looking into the living room and seeing that dog inside the house. Their kindness was tempered with the sting of social order, racism, and White supremacy.

ID Please

I think about how it felt to be a graduate student in the Augusta University library at 10pm frantically trying to complete a paper before the deadline and being approached by campus security and told that if I could not produce an ID I would have to leave. Common sense policing and mutual respect is all we ask. Why not ask me to produce some other form of proof that I'm a student such as a registration email, class schedule, etc? It's in those moments that we feel as if we are in the burning house, and no one else notices. These unnecessary moments also fuel the ongoing resentment that exists between law enforcement and the African-American community.

Are You the Janitor?

During my second year as a principal I was at the building on a Saturday afternoon. My car was the only one in the parking lot. As I walked up the empty hallway, I saw the Orkin exterminator turn the corner and head in my direction. He was a middle-aged Asian man. We greeted one another and the first question he asked me was "Are you the janitor?". In a school with over 80 staff members, why would his first assumption be that I was the janitor? Couldn't I have been one of the teachers or maybe the principal or assistant principal? It's in moments like this that we experience the micro-aggressions that remind us that we are in a burning house in American society.

The Right Conversation

In discussing this issue with a close friend who is also a school principal, she shared how she tells her son that he needs to "work harder than everyone else" as an African-American boy. I understand her intent, but the reality is that Ahmaud Arbery wasn't murdered for not working hard. George Floyd wasn't murdered for lack of effort. Sandra Bland wasn't killed for failing to put her best foot forward. I don't want our youth to be disillusioned into thinking that education and a strong work ethic will provide immunity from the smoke that is engulfing African-Americans in this country. Yes, we should instill a solid work ethic in our kids, but that is an entirely separate conversation from the one of having access to basic human rights and dignity in the workplace and society. Our kids need survival skills. They need to understand their rights, and the history of struggle that does not appear in our history texts. We must demand that the conversation about cultural responsiveness drill down to what resources are purchased and what events are included in the standards placed before our children.

Nearly every African-American man you know can share his own list of moments when he was reminded that the house is still burning. Just ask him. My point is that this is not a recent set of events, this has been our collective lived experience. There's smoke. Thick smoke. Others see it now. I'm tired of trying to convince them that the house has been burning for years. Toxic smoke. I'm tired of talking and pointing towards the flames. My focus now is on working with a team of educators willing to do the heavy lifting of preparing a generation of youth to reconstruct our society. It's your turn to talk. I can't breathe.

Chapter 11: What's Good

I T WAS AN UNUSUALLY BRISK APRIL AFTERNOON IN LITHONIA. OUR BEDROOM WINDOW IS OPEN WIDE, ALLOWING A CHILLY BREEZE TO WAFT INTO THE BEDROOM. I'M READING "I CHOOSE TO STAY: A BLACK TEACHER REFUSES TO DESERT THE INNER CITY" BY SALOME THOMAS-EL. Throughout the book, Principal El shares stories of building relationships with students, teaching them chess, life-skills, and about their history. I revisited the book because of a FB post by one of my former students, Juawn Jackson, who mentioned his experience in my classroom as a 5th grader twenty years ago, learning to play chess.

That well-mannered and curious student went on to become a teacher and is now running for a seat on the local school board in Macon, Georgia. He reminds me that our success is not solely measured by assessment scores, but by the trajectories we set in place with our work with young people. Those are the success stories I share when people ask me "What's Good" in public education.

I'd just finished a call with my performance coach, Mrs. Sharper, who reminded me that what we all need now is to take a moment to acknowledge "what's good". She encouraged me to take the time to pause and soak in "what's good" at Marbut Traditional Theme School. As she is sharing that statement, I'm thinking about how much I appreciate my team of teachers who understand the role they play in the lives of our students and families. Outside the window I hear the voices of children playing and riding their bikes up and down the sidewalk. I've missed hearing those voices in the hallways of our school, so I found it a welcome break in the deafening silence of social distancing. It reminds me of what I often tell my leadership team: *In every crisis and conflict, we have to dig deep to find the lesson and discover **what's good** about a given circumstance. It's always there, we just have to be able to pause long enough to see it.*

What's Good! It is a layered, two-word phrase that is triune in its connotation: one-part greeting, one-part question, and one-part call to action. A cursory glance at a social media stream leaves us all questioning what's happening at the highest levels of our government, inciting us to challenge and question national priorities during a global emergency, but most importantly we have finally begun to acknowledge the contributions of those who provide essential services that support our children and families in this nation.

Acknowledgement

In my city and for much of my generation, "What's good" is a phrase expressed to acknowledge someone as you encounter them in person or as you initiate an informal chat. You are essentially saying, "I see you". Next week, we will celebrate Teacher Appreciation Week 2020 and we must take a moment to acknowledge what's good in our public education system. The theme for this week's virtual staff meeting was "What's Good?". I wanted to take an hour to acknowledge and celebrate the work of our team in the midst of the sudden shift to virtual learning. In doing so, the first group I wanted to tap into was my dedicated parents who have been key players in setting the stage for virtual learning in support of our teachers. Via text, I asked our parents at every grade level to send me an email sharing stories of teachers who have gone above and beyond since school closures began. I wanted to shed light on the calls, the follow-up calls, the video lessons, and troubleshooting that often goes on without accolades or acknowledgement. I sent the text at 10:45am. For the next several hours there was a consistent stream of emails from parents sharing their appreciation for the work of teachers. After all of the emails were compiled into one document, we had 10 pages of messages from families about specific teachers and their dedication to this work pre and post pandemic.

> "I would sincerely like to take Mrs. Crowe-Harris for her dedication to her students. Mrs. Crowe-Harris goes above and beyond. During this unusual time, I feel as though my baby has not missed a beat and that is thanks to Mrs. Crowe Harris. We still have assignments, individual sessions, and fun activities. In addition, Mrs. Crowe-Harris sends EXTRA resources for our children. I am just grateful that my baby has a teacher that is true and dedicated to her calling. I cannot thank you enough. "

I compiled all of the messages and sent them to teachers as a link. It was a small gesture that meant much to those who have given much.

Questioning and Confronting

In the more literal sense, "What's Good" is posing a direct question that begs an answer. Educational leaders understand that working within the system means that we must sometimes confront the very system we work within. We have to 'rage against the machine' when it does not work in the best interest of the communities we serve. Like most educators, I've been looking at the void in leadership from our nation's Secretary of Education during the most pivotal crisis for public education of the century. Like those voices from outside my window, Dr. Salome Thomas-El and Dr. Shango Blake are the voices emerging from within public education, shattering the deafening silence, at once acknowledging us and challenging us to act.

Last year, the parent of one of my students introduced me to the work of Dr. Shango Blake. As a principal and now as an educational consultant, Dr. Blake is a champion for public education and for Hip-Hop culture. His show, The Classroom Hip Hop 101 is just one example of the work he is doing to reshape the landscape of education at the grassroots level. I was immediately impressed by the way he approaches his work with schools to confront inequities and disparities that do a disservice for students in urban schools. During this national shift to virtual learning, Dr.

Blake is working with communities to support parents and educators by hosting parent/teacher check-ins on Fridays.

The challenges of leading a school community virtually require 'out of the box' thinking. In every challenge, there is an opportunity to improve and explore and find what's good. What's good is that with tenacity and faith I was able to contact both Dr. Thomas-El and Dr. Blake and encourage them to join our weekly virtual staff meeting as special guests this week. They poured into my staff, sharing concern, providing inspiration and a historical context to our present circumstances. Teacher-leaders shared what's good from their respective grade levels, celebrating one another and breakthroughs with students. The common thread in what was shared on that call is that we have to take care of ourselves in order to take care of our families and students. We must be there for one another during these times of isolation. With education conferences cancelled, we managed to have our own mini-conference with the assistance of two educational giants acknowledging us and confronting us under the premise of two-words: What's Good.

Chapter 12: Let's Be Frank

I'S DR. SEUSS DAY AT LARCHMONT ELEMENTARY IN 2016. WE ARE IN EAST TACOMA, A GRITTY NEIGHBORHOOD WITH INDUSTRIAL ROOTS. OUR STUDENTS' PARENTS ARE A MIX OF IMMIGRANTS, TACOMA NATIVES, AND TOUGH WORKING-CLASS FAMILIES. In 25 minutes or so, the dismissal bell will ring, and hundreds of students will pour out of our doors into the surrounding streets. A fortunate fold of students will board the bus driven by the man who has just walked into the front office wearing a Seuss hat and red bowtie. With a booming baritone laugh, he greets the office staff and beams with excitement about the school-wide celebration of Dr. Seuss. On this afternoon, he's brought a book that he wants to read to a class later in the week.

Mr. Shepherd wasn't like the bus drivers I'd encounter as a classroom teacher on bus duty or walking my kids to a bus in the afternoon. He was composed. He wasn't frazzled. His calmness and enthusiasm infused the students with a similar calmness. I can't count the number of times I saw him give out stuffed animals to kindergartners who had a tough day. Mr. Shepherd was the opposite of what I recall from my own childhood. The bus drivers I remember started the day barking out orders. "Sit down! Get your feet out of the aisle!" The only time they walked into the school's front office was to deliver a discipline report to the school principal.

The millions of people who support public education in school cafeterias, school buses, and in custodial roles are an extension of work of classroom teachers and principals. They too embrace our kids and create spaces where they are celebrated and nurtured. All too often, we overlook their contributions. But every once in a while, someone comes along and reminds us of the potential for creating magic beyond the classroom. Mr. Shepherd guides us there.

Over the twenty years that I've worked in and around public schools, I've only encountered a few people who had the remarkable ability to instantly change the temperature in a room. They were individuals with larger than life personalities that radiated around them, infusing every project they touched with an air of alchemy. Mr. Shepherd was the only one I'd ever met with this gift who was not an educator by trade. Each afternoon he held court either from the door of his bus or from the driver's seat. High-fives, handshakes, questions about the day. He did what we begged teachers to do at the start of their day. Our students were his students, but we too were students of his. Each afternoon he was teaching us powerful lessons about the energy of enthusiasm, the hope embedded in humor, and centrality of celebrations.

"Mr. Mountain, I've got an idea. Listen...I want to bring ice cream for everyone on my bus. They've been doing much better and I want to celebrate them. What do you think?"

Like a teacher devising ways to reshape the culture in a classroom, Mr. Shepherd is always looking for and recognizing the small successes and incremental wins that so many of us overlook.

Frank Shepherd is an icon. Gregarious. Attuned. He is the default master of ceremonies for hundreds of children each day as they ride his bus through the streets of Tacoma, Washington. For the fortunate, he is the first face of Tacoma Public Schools that many children see as they venture out of their neighborhoods. He sets the tone for the day for hundreds of young scholars before they ever venture through the front doors of a school. The poetic irony of his last name, 'Shepherd', is apropos to who he is and what he does. A shepherd watches over a flock during the day, ensuring that none of them go astray. Shepherds are found leading their flock out early in the mornings and bringing them back home in the evenings to a place of comfort and safety.

Frank Shepherd is not a fictional character. He is the personification of the idea of leading from anywhere in an organization. Months after I departed Washington State to take a role as a principal in metro-Atlanta, Mr. Shepherd found me on Facebook and took the time to extend his congratulations to me and my family. If we are to continue to transform our communities when school resumes, it will take everyone involved to be a little more like "Frank". Let's be "Frank" in how we interact with our scholars, colleagues and parents. The Bureau of Labor Statistics reports that there are over 681,000 school bus drivers in the United States. Just imagine the impact that could be made in our communities if they all were a bit more like "Frank". Bus drivers, secretaries, school nurses, paraprofessionals, cafeteria staff, custodians all add value to the work we do by way of their daily interactions with our scholars. The questions they pose matter. The compliments they give boost confidence and self-esteem. Mr. Shepherd is the first and last school employee his students encounter each day. He reminds us that each day is a new journey and, frankly speaking, we are all in the driver's seat.

Chapter 13: Keep You Posted

WALKING THROUGH WATER FOR LEADERS MEANS MANAGING PEOPLE WELL. THIS CAN BE A CHALLENGE AS MANAGING PEOPLE IS MUCH MORE COMPLEX THAN MANAGING A CLASSROOM OF CHILDREN. Those of us who have chosen education as our profession come into this work with many different life experiences perspectives about race and work ethics. While some choose a long workday with evening hours in the classroom wrapping up or preparing for the next day others leave within minutes after their required work hours. School closures have me thinking about what I miss about being around my staff and students. I've resorted to creating new routines and structures to keep myself mentally engaged and productive. My school family keeps me smiling and laughing about the beauty of life. The first question of the day was usually, "Did you get my text? I sent it this morning." If I checked my phone every time I received a text I wouldn't get anything done. Most principals receive dozens of emails and texts each day so finding the time to filter through what's important and what can wait takes time and a system. The messages, emails and phone calls about why folks can't come to work always seem to end with the same hopeful phrase: "Will keep you posted."

Teachers who find the humor in the job are less likely to be consumed by the emotional stress of being the sole adult in the room with 30 children. Principals need to laugh too! The responsibilities of running a school can seem overwhelming. Some principals take themselves so seriously that they mute their own joy and the joy of those around them. The ability to laugh and enjoy those unforgettable moments, mining them for lessons, is precisely how we keep going. Moving into the principalship has its humorous moments because adults can become as creative in their reasons for either not arriving on time or taking days off. Research shows that teacher attendance and student performance go hand in hand. That's why schools look for ways to incentivize good attendance and punctuality. Standing alongside the millions of punctual and professional educators is another group of creatives. Every school has these creatives who, like true artists, have trouble getting to the venue on time: the consistently late, the frequently absent, and the early departures.

The Two-Step

If nothing else, Mrs. Stevens is consistent. She seems to copy and paste the same text message to me every other week with only slightly different phrasing? I'm a writer, so all I ask is for a bit of originality and creativity in your approach to this process. Her approach is well thought out. Mrs. Stevens is the inventor of 'the two step approach' of calling out from work. It typically starts the night before. Mrs. Stevens sends the text with so much detail that I'd rather not read as I'm trying to get to other urgent messages coming in simultaneously. The text is nearly as long as this blog post. Seriously. "Had a late night last night. April's fever was over 100. She is my middle child. Tried to get her to rest, first upstairs, then downstairs where it is cooler. My mother in law, who lives in Gwinnett County near the Mall of Georgia is coming over to help once morning traffic dies down. 85 can be thick in the morning." Then, without fail, the morning text arrives. "My daughter isn't feeling well this morning. Temp is still high, so I won't be in today. Will keep you posted."

The Cliffhanger

Mr. Collier is one of the greatest literary minds of our time. He would make a great screenwriter for Tyler Perry films because his reasons for not coming to work are sheer creative genius. His mind is fertile ground for the most imaginative scenarios for not being able to come in. Once, after days of not reporting to work, he sent a text apologizing and informed us that he'd been hospitalized. Mr. Collier's excuses are action packed with riveting cliffhangers. They are interspersed with interesting characters that pull you into the plot. My phone rings and the voice on the other end shouts through the sound of cars passing by, "Mr. Mountain, I was on my way to work and about a mile before I got there my tire blew out. I'm out here now waiting on the tow truck. I don't think I'm gonna make it in today, but if I can I will let you know." The next week I get a text, "My uncle Ephram just arrived from a military mission in China and he has lost his luggage at the airport. I went to pick him up, but we have now been detained by customs." He pauses for a few moments, then writes: "Will keep you posted."

The Appliance Warehouse

Mrs. Mims must have a magnificent home because it seems that her approach to not coming to work always centers around the delivery of some type of appliance. If there is a staff meeting, Mrs. Mims has to leave early so that they can deliver her dryer. If there is a teacher workday, Mrs. Mims has to come in later so that they can install the new deep freezer. Observation scheduled? Sorry, that's the day the water heater is being delivered and they can only come sometime between 10am and 2pm. I swear she must have a washer, dryer and stove in every room of her house because the deliveries have been consistent for three years. If it's a 3-day weekend, Mrs. Mims returns a day later because the only day they could bring the new refrigerator is the Monday we are scheduled to return. But she always leaves hope that she can get things adjusted. "I was trying to get this rescheduled outside the workday, but so far the only times they have available are Monday between 9am and 3pm. Will keep you posted."

School of Dentistry

Wednesdays at 2:45 are designated as staff meeting days. We all agreed that we would keep this as our consistent date to avoid scheduling conflicts. Mr. Wilson always had something urgent to tell me at the beginning of the meeting or midway through. He'd get my attention, wave me over, then whisper, "I need to go to a dentist appointment". "No problem. Take care." It took me a while to pick up on the pattern, but it happened week after week after week. On this day, the meeting had begun, and another staff member was presenting. I see Mr. Wilson gathering his things to leave about 30 minutes into the meeting. I rush over to the door and ask, "Are you leaving?" He says, "Yes, I have a dental appointment." "Again? It seems like you have all of your dental appointments on Wednesdays. You know we agreed that this was our meeting date. Can you get it changed?" He smiled slightly as a person does when the jig is up, looked at his watch and said, "I'll try to get it changed for next time. Will keep you posted."

Catch Me If You Can

Ms. Wrigley is one of our best teachers. She is talented, reflective and always looking for ways to improve her every move in the classroom. I rarely get texts from her or emails about being late or having to leave early. But, if I announce that visitors are coming to do walkthroughs on a specific date, Ms. Wrigley will politely inform me that she will be out on that date due to an appointment. I might see her in the hallway and say, "Hey, I'm gonna come by today to see that guided reading lesson." Best believe that they will be at recess or on a library visit or restroom break. Ms. Wrigley avoids being observed at all costs. Like any principal, I'd share with my staff if a district team was coming to do a walkthrough on a certain day. I'd remind them of our non-negotiables with the hopes that they would be at the top of their game. Ms. Wrigley wasn't planning to even come to the game. So it it was time for me to check in on that guided reading lesson I told her I was coming to observe. I grabbed my rolling cart, laptop and cell phone and headed toward her classroom. After walking all around the school looking for Ms. Wrigley and her class, I find them in the rear of the school doing a science experiment. I look on from a distance, wondering why the schedule changed. She pauses, looks up at me and says, "We decided to get in a little Science today since it's nice out." I smile and nod in agreement about the weather. She looks at her students as they look around the lawn for a certain type of leaf. I ask, "So when will the reading lesson be tomorrow?" She takes a deep breath and says, "Should be around 10, but you know we have testing and project presentations. Will keep you posted."

The Big Payback

Mrs. Olson ran a tight ship. She demanded respect from her students and operated her classroom with military precision. Students feared her, as did some of the staff. Underneath the tough exterior was a soft-hearted woman with a good heart. I began to notice that she was in constant conflict with her colleagues and parents. I was receiving many emails from parents complaining about her approach. I decided to take a closer look at the culture of the classroom. After a few observation cycles, I pinpointed some of the things that were undermining her work with students and families. The approach, the tone, the rigidity. But as I began sharing my observations, I quickly realized that Mrs. Olson hated constructive feedback. She only wanted to hear what went well and that was it. No matter how positively it was framed or how soft the landing of the suggestion, she despised being told what might improve her lesson or the culture of her classroom. If I had to discuss a parent complaint with Mrs. Olson, I was 99% certain that she was going to take the next several days off. As I planned the meeting with her, I'd just tell my AP to go ahead and prepare to secure a substitute for the classroom for a few days. Her emails were five paragraph long and winding treatises about being undermined by parents, students and staff. In her mind, the ultimate payback was to inconvenience us all by not coming to work. Securing effective substitutes could be a challenge for us and she was well aware of that. I always wondered if she realized that in doing this she was also undermining her level of student achievement, something she took great pride in. Naturally, in her absence parents inquired about what was going on. When will she return? Is she okay? I had no definitive answers. I'd reach out to Mrs. Olson to "check in" to see how she was doing. "Hope you are feeling better. Any idea when you will return?" A few hours pass and I get a reply, "Waiting on the doctors to let me know. Will keep you posted."

The Undertaker

Mrs. Edwards was either a member of a very large family or the central figure in an organized crime syndicate. It seemed that every other month she had to take time off to go to assist with the funeral arrangements of another family member. Not only was she attending the funeral service, she was playing a key role in the planning of the services, which required even more days away from work. I contemplated calling law enforcement. How could so much death surround one person. Was she...? Obituary after obituary rolled in as confirmation of deaths. I felt sorry for this woman. I think some family members even died multiple times. "On behalf of the school, please extend our condolences to your family. When is the funeral?", I'd ask. "Well, we are still making the arrangements. This has hit us all hard. I don't know when I'll be able to come back. Will keep you posted."

Principals don't get the calls about absences and texts about running late now that schools are closed. It feels like the world as we knew it is now closed. When school reopens, I can't wait to get my first call or text from a member of my team after having been out of school for months. I wonder who it will be and what will be the reason. Who's sick? What new appliance is being delivered during school hours? Who is being laid to rest (again)? After this we could all use a good laugh. That text or email is coming, I can feel it. Will keep you posted.

The year was 1960. The scent of coffee and flavored sodas hovered in the air as five young men gathered to discuss the sit-ins that were occurring in North Carolina. This conversation among determined young people in Atlanta was the humble beginning of a movement. The setting was the Young & Milton Drug Store near the campus of Clark College, now Clark Atlanta University. The movement would later be led by a very young Martin Luther King, Jr. What was it about Dr. Martin Luther King Jr. that made him a transformational leader? Sonia Thompson tackles this question in her article Three Skills Martin Luther King Mastered to Become a Transformational Leader. She points to his empathy, his hunger to learn more, and his courage to speak up when no one else would or when silence was the easiest option. Tough times require courageous conversations. Members of any company, organization, or school community have to ask themselves the question: Are you along for the ride or are you really onboard? What's your level of commitment to the work that's laid out before us? This group of activists would face being spat upon, attacked by dogs, struck with police batons, and arrested. When the challenges come along, and they will, those who are not fully committed will stand on the sidelines and watch as the plan falls apart. They are prepared to use the emergency exits at the first sign of trouble. Those who are fully onboard will do everything in their power to uplift the vision, support the plan, and troubleshoot the roadblocks.

I imagine where we'd be now as a nation if those involved in the Civil Rights Movement of the 1960's couldn't be civil enough with one another to organize protests. What would have happened if their movement was derailed by infighting and those who had opposing viewpoints to King's non-violent philosophy decided to take a different approach. I believe that what we are currently seeing in public education is our modern-day version of the civil rights movement.

- Charter schools and private schools are offering parents additional options and pulling federal funds away from public schools.
- District lines are being redrawn based on new subdivisions and the corresponding incomes as neighborhoods become more gentrified.
- School districts are demanding greater accountability for student progress, leading some educators to reposition themselves in more affluent areas to ensure they avoid certain challenges.
- Parents want to be advocates for their children but don't know which fights to fight and when to fight them.

The well organized protests that took place throughout the Civil Rights Movement took a great deal of planning and commitment on the part of the participants. When the sheriff shouted that the protesters would all be arrested, no one said a word. They all stopped and knelt to pray.

Those chosen to do the work of changing the status quo had to possess a certain temperament to resist the urge to "fight fire with fire" when confronted by screaming protesters. They were taunted and provoked in practice settings to prepare them for the hurl of insults, slurs, and intimidation that would be thrust upon them during the actual protests. Ironically, principals find themselves on the receiving end of much of the frustration and rage that parents hold for public education. Threats, defamation of character, name calling, and blatant disrespect have become par for the course in a society that no longer views the profession with the level of respect and esteem it once held. Somewhere along the way, we've come to view educators as 'workers' undeserving of respect rather than educated professionals. This needs to change. The people to whom we entrust our children for 7-8 hours a day deserve our utmost respect

Recently, I sat in a PTA Executive Committee meeting with a team of six parents from 6:00pm until 8:30. Despite being tired from full-time jobs, they'd committed to work out the details of our plans for the year. Helping more parents transition from riding to being fully onboard is a task not for the faint of heart. I recently read the King Philosophy, which includes his description of the 3 evils, poverty, racism, and militarism. Most importantly here, he lays out his six steps of non-violent social change:

1. Investigation
2. Education
3. Personal Commitment
4. Discussion/Negotiation
5. Direct Action
6. Reconciliation

Everyone engaged in this work needs to revisit step 3, asking the very question posed in the title: Onboard or just riding? The discussion and negotiation phase is where we begin to shift the tide and get more people on board with changing public education collectively with parents and teachers working alongside one another. We are actively working within the profession to level the playing field to ensure that schools and families located in communities that are predominantly African-American have access to the same high standards of education that students in more affluent areas experience. Access and exposure is a civil right. This is a task not for the faint of heart. It has been described as a thankless job, but that is actually a misnomer considering the fact that I'm stopped several times each day by parents wanting to express their sincere thanks for the work that my teachers and I do for their children. We are not discouraged by the challenges but encouraged by those who are fully onboard pushing us to keep driving forward.

Chapter 14: Jazz Improvisation and Public Education

URIOUS. ECLECTIC YET GROUNDED. ALWAYS SLIGHTLY OFF BEAT. THELONIOUS MONK IS ARGUABLY ONE OF THE GREATEST JAZZ MUSICIANS WHO EVER GRACED THE PIANO. His penchant for dancing around the stage in the throes of the music enchanted audiences. His effortless style, both musical and aesthetic, influenced the direction of the genre. Monk is the embodiment of the attributes I seek when looking for new educators to join our team. Much mythology surrounds Monk, lingering over his legacy like clouds of smoke in a jazz club, casting shadows of naivety and madness.

"Thelonious Monk possessed an impressive knowledge of, and appreciation for, Western classical music, not to mention an encyclopedic knowledge of hymns and gospel music, American popular songs, and a variety of obscure art songs that defy categorization", writes Robin D.G. Kelley, author of *Thelonious Monk: The Life and Times of An American Original*. Kelley takes jazz enthusiasts well beyond the liner notes into the meandering life of an aptly termed "American original". In doing so, he reminds me of the challenge principals and leadership teams face each year as they work to staff their schools with the right mix of talents and temperaments. Public education in America is in dire need of more 'originals. We need a teaching force with the ability to improvise like jazz musicians and sway with changes in the composition while onstage. They need to be ready to use their art and chosen profession to shape society for the better.

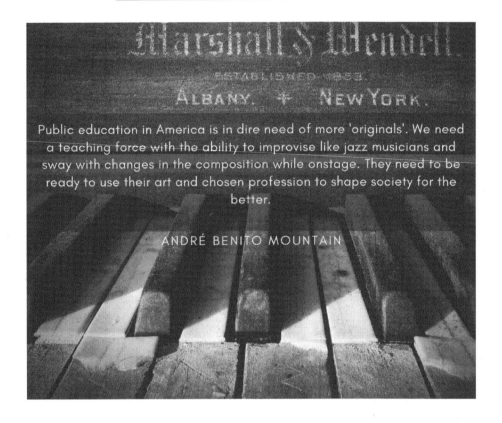

Public education in America is in dire need of more 'originals'. We need a teaching force with the ability to improvise like jazz musicians and sway with changes in the composition while onstage. They need to be ready to use their art and chosen profession to shape society for the better.

ANDRÉ BENITO MOUNTAIN

I was recently asked, "What are the factors you consider when undertaking school staffing?" My approach to staffing has changed over time from small, intimate interviews to a more open process which includes a broader sampling from my staff to assist in selecting candidates. Personally, I look for five attributes in candidates:

1. The ability to improvise
2. Broad exposure
3. Reflectiveness
4. Social justice leanings
5. Readiness to adapt

Improvise

The term 'jazz improvisation' can be applied to the art of teaching in the sense that it requires adjustments and a level of skill that is acquired over time. Jazz improvisation does not mean musicians are simply making it up as they go along. They all know the tune and the role of their instrument, but they fully embrace the flexibility of the moment and play in that manner. In the same vein as jazz improvisation pulls on the creativity of the participants, the art of teaching is neither formulaic nor random. It compels us to channel our passions, merge them with the interests of our students and our content in a way that creates magic.

Pull from everywhere

What are you plugged into that influences your approach to instruction? What ignites you from within? The articles, books and videos that inform our practice help us to continue evolving as educators. Educators must make the time to continue reading broadly. While formal education is necessary for earning credentials and certification, I would suggest that self-education is the most important education we can receive. The best teachers have interests as broad as Monk's musical influences. Reading broadly on a range of topics adds immensely to a tool kit that students will inevitably ask you to pull from with questions about global warming, politics, or the arts.

Be Reflective

Watching videos of Monk in rehearsals making adjustments to the tempo of a piece, and occasionally arguing with bandmates reveal a level of dedication to the craft. The varying temperaments, egos and levels of expertise on a team can become a challenge when it's time to collaborate. When we care about the finished product, we devote the time to practice, reflect, study and adjust. Tell me about a time a lesson didn't go as planned and how you adjusted it or retaught the material? In co-planning, how do you work through conflict? What can you offer our team?

Fight for something

Teachers joining an instructional team, especially in urban settings, need to be willing to fight for something that matters. There are many wars to be won and education has become the front-line of sorts for the fight for human rights, civil rights and equity. Understanding this and being willing to confront and grapple with this on a daily basis is what it means to be the type of warrior teacher that changes student trajectories. Nina Simone was as much of an American original as Thelonious Monk. While other singers tried to mirror the sound of their contemporaries, her tone was unlike anyone else's. In the case of Nina, the social climate of the 1960's called for a level of artistic courage that Nina was built for since her early years in South Carolina. Nina fully embraced her culture and understood that her embrace of her culture had implications for people of color around the world. Her hairstyles, her jewelry, her attire and the content of her lyrics represented the full spectrum of her gospel, soul, and jazz roots in the American South. She realized the powerful role of the influence of artistic interpretations a society in flux. She recorded songs like "I Wish I Knew How It Would Feel to Be Free" and "Young Gifted and Black" that gained critical acclaim and provided a soundtrack to a social movement. In 1967, Nina Simone released the album "Nina Simone – High Priestess of Soul". On the back of the album, the Del Shields describes Nina in this manner:

> "Songwriters who write songs with a message, because they feel that survival is based on truth, seek her out. And she records their material. Many times she has suffered the banishment of her tunes by the archaic censors who fear to upset the establishment. On occasion she has become the center of controversy because she demands first-rate

conditions in order to perform at her maximum degree of excellence for her audience. And this is Nina."

Be Ye Ready

For two years I traveled to schools alongside a talented group of jazz musicians presenting a program called "Taking Notes: Jazz and the American Story". The band consisted of Karen Gordon on piano, Joe Collier on trumpet, Dave Weston on bass, Not Gaddy on drums, and Jimmy Easton on saxophone. The program chronicled American history and how it was reflected in the evolution of Jazz music from the 1800's through present times. My role was to provide a story telling component at intervals between the songs. When we faced time constraints or tech issues, we'd make slight changes in the set list and the audiences never knew we were improvising. The best musicians, like the best teachers, are always ready for a change in plans. Demonstrating flexibility in the face of change has meant much more in recent weeks with school closures and virtual learning taking center stage in public education.

When educators study the genre of jazz, we learn about its African roots, we learn about how musical styles develop over time, and we learn about freedom. Jazz teaches us that truth can't be muted. It teaches us that even in the bluest moment, there is something to celebrate. It teaches us the value of being unscripted. Send me the American originals! I am seeking out American originals to join our school. I want to hear from someone who failed at delivering a lesson and revised it and came back stronger. I want to hear from someone who speaks truth and authenticity and doesn't sprinkle their narrative with politically correct catch phrases like "life-long learning", "all students can learn", "no child left behind" and "free and reduced". Ours is a profession battling a psychometric obsession with sorting and organizing. Students and adults would do well to heed the advice of Thelonious Monk: "The genius is the one most like himself."

Chapter 15: Stepping Out of the Boat

"Come," he said. Then Peter got down out of the boat, walked on the water and came toward Jesus. But when he saw the wind, he was afraid and, beginning to sink, cried out, "Lord, save me!" Immediately Jesus reached out his hand and caught him. "You of little faith," he said, "why did you doubt?"

– Matthew 14: 29-31

WHO KNEW THAT BEING A PRINCIPAL COULD BE SO STRESSFUL? LIKE MOST PRINCIPALS, I ENTERED THE ROLE WITH A BELIEF THAT THE PEOPLE I WOULD BE SERVING WOULD WELCOME MY APPROACH TO LEADERSHIP WITH OPEN ARMS. That **does** happen on many occasions. You can read stories and FB posts about the joys of leading. They are all true. But there are other stories to be told about leadership that I would like for aspiring leaders to know so they will be prepared for what the role truly entails. There are moments when you have to remind yourself that you are not part of an action film where the script is written in a way where your livelihood is threatened, your reputation is attacked, and people you trusted in your inner circle betray you in critical moments. The plot has multiple sinister twists that can't be predicted. There are tense meetings, long conference calls, angry parents, difficult staff members, shortages of resources, and the ever-present push to increase student achievement. There are triumphant tales of overcoming and miraculous saves where the underdogs come out on top. In the book of Matthew we read the account of Jesus appearing to men in a boat while they are surrounded by a brutal storm. Peter says to Jesus, "Lord, if it is you, command me to come to you on the water." After he gives the command, Peter steps out of the boat, on faith, and begins to walk on water. Only when he looks around at the storm surrounding them does he begin to doubt and sink. He had enough faith to step out of the boat and walk on water briefly, but he became distracted by everything happening around him that he quickly began to sink. Like a courageous and well-intentioned school leader, Peter had enough faith to take steps forward while everyone else remained in the safety and comfort of the boat.

Lesson 1: It takes faith to take the first step

Though he was criticized for having "little faith" that eventually led to his sinking, he had to have some faith to even take the first step. In examining this account from the lens of a school leader, I see the many times I criticized my leaders for their missteps in the midst of a raging storm. Never forget that it takes enormous courage and faith to assume the responsibility for a school. Over the years, I've been absolutely guilty of holding my leaders up for scrutiny, but I had no idea how much they were balancing all while living their lives beyond the school. Every principal has a shelf filled with books on leadership and best practices in public education. We pull from business texts on team building and books of motivational quotes. We draw from multiple sources to charge ourselves up so that we can energize those we lead each day. Within months of taking on my role as principal, I realized that like Peter, principals don't walk on water. *They walk through it!*

I was determined to lead my school in the way I wanted schools to be led when I was a 5th grade teacher at Monte Sano Elementary in Augusta. I wanted to close the door to room 216, teach my 24 students, and go home to my wife and infant daughter. My interactions with the principal were limited. Why? Our roles were so different, and my job was to teach my kids, not to assist in leading the direction of the school. I wanted to stay in my lane, and I appreciated the fact that she stayed in hers. When she gave our grade level a task, we figured out how to get it done without any pushback. We wanted her to be pleased with our work and our level of commitment to her leadership. Now, we did have our share of difficult parents who seemed to find the proverbial fly in every bowl of soup we served. But we were usually able to appease these parents with a few explanations and reasonable adjustments.

Lesson 2: Fear will sink you

The daily walk of being a principal in an urban school comes with the expectation that we can literally step out of the boat and walk on water in the midst of a storm. Peter's fear caused him to sink. The best leaders can become captives to their own forms of fear. Education is a very political profession and principals naturally think long and hard about how the decisions they make will potentially impact their career trajectory. I've found that those who truly make a lasting impact in the profession operate from a place that is far removed from this fear of failure. They move with confidence and always in the best interest of the students they serve.

What would surprise most people about the role of the principal is the number of people who actively hurl threats at you about what they will do if they don't get their way. Everyone seems to have an agenda either for their own interest or that of their child. Sometimes those agendas are great in that they provide a benefit for the entire school in the form of a strategic partnership or a school-wide event that all students can enjoy. Things take a turn when policies are enforced, because inevitably some parents take issue with the policies applying to their child. On the one hand, we have parents who want strict enforcement of policies against other people's children, but when their child commits an infraction, they want to suggest that the teacher or the school has a vendetta out against their seven-year-old child.

Should I Call the Board?

Ayana was one of the unruliest students in the 4th grade. Her father, Mr. Watkins, was in law enforcement and while he understood that she was a very difficult child, he always attacked the school when we held her accountable for being rude, uncooperative, or disrespectful to teachers and her peers. His favorite line was, "Do I need to call the Board?". I'd heard it more times than I cared to remember. It was a veiled attempt to issue direct threat to our due process and to my leadership. The comment was hurled at teachers and at me during conference calls. On this particular day, Ayana had been very rude to her Spanish teacher and refused to follow any directives that were given. I called Mr. Watkins as my assistant principal sat in my office. I placed the phone on speaker. I explained to Mr. Watkins that we had issued Ayana one day in ISS and she refused to go. I explained to him that her refusal would result in an out-of-school suspension if she did not comply. "I didn't get a write up...now do I have to go to the board to get a write up?" Here we were again with the veiled threats. I said, "Mr. Watkins, you have every right to contact the board, but let's not continue to move away from the issue at hand. The real issue is your daughter not complying with school and district policies. You continue to bring up this idea of calling the board when we have these discussions and I want you to know that it does not change our level of expectations. I am going to continue to hold Ayana accountable." He paused and said, "Mr. Mountain, I don't have a problem with you, I'm just frustrated with the system." He then apologized and continued the conversation in a much more sensible tone. Confronting the threat directly as opposed to ignoring it seemed to deflate the power of it instantly.

I Shall Not Be Moved

Ms. Brinks had 3 sons who attended our school. Whenever she came to the school, her mother was always present and did most of the talking. Ms. Brinks just looked on with a scowl, never saying too much until she just couldn't contain her emotions anymore. When this happened, we'd witness her emotional outburst and talk her through it. She was the parent who wanted what she wanted when she wanted it without regard to processes and procedures. On this busy afternoon, we were managing our dismissal line in the front of the school. There were over 200 cars on a typical day coming through the front circle. She pulls up in a red sedan, parks in the circle and gets out of the car. She storms into the front office, ignoring the fact that her car is now impeding the traffic of our dismissal process. Once in the office, she begins to demand to know where her oldest son is, forgetting that he's signed up for tutoring on Tuesday afternoons and is in a tutoring session. My staff assures her that we will find him and send him to the front. We ask her to please move her vehicle so we can continue with our dismissal process. She says, "I ain't movin' my car till yall find my child". My assistant principal offers to move the car for her while she waits inside. She refuses.

The next day the saga continues as we receive a call from the district because the parent has filed a complaint saying we were "extremely rude to her". Now, instead of meeting with the teachers I'd planned to meet with to discuss instruction or returning calls from parents, I'm gathering the statements from witnesses so that we can provide a narrative of what actually happened in the front office the previous afternoon. I'm asked to call the parent back and to discuss the incident. I agree to make the call because I'm hopeful that she had calmed down and is in a completely different emotional space. That was not to be the case. As I open the call I ask, "Ms. Brinks, is there something I can do to assist. I know we had an issue yesterday at the car-rider circle and I just wanted to reach out. Is everything okay?". She says, "No, it's not okay. I have an issue with Mrs. Brant and I don't want her on car rider duty in the afternoons. She doesn't know how to talk to people. She wasn't professional." She goes on to say that Mrs. Brant asked her to move her vehicle, as she should have. Now the parent is demanding that I remove Mrs. Brant from this duty station so that she does not have to interact with her. She then said, "Am I gonna have to call your supervisor?" In my mind I'm thinking, "How in the hell does she have the nerve to demand changes in our duty schedule? You were the one who left your car in a loading area, but now you're making demands of us. Unbelievable." But I couldn't say this because it would not be the politically correct thing to say. I had to keep my head in the game. I had to be diplomatic...*as long as I could*. It tried, believe me I tried. But I'm not perfect. I'm human and I can only take so much. So then I say, "I understand you were looking for your son and we put the wheels in motion to find him. He was in tutoring. But Ms. Brinks, let me be clear, you were wrong to leave your vehicle in the circle during dismissal. It was uncalled for and Mrs. Brant did her job and asked you to please move your vehicle. I asked and my assistant principal asked. Now you are asking me if you should call my supervisor. That doesn't frighten me at all. I stand behind how we handled things yesterday and I hope you understand that we will not change our processes intended to protect children for your convenience. So make the calls you need to make, because we are going to continue to work in the best interest of our students." My assistant principal looked like she was about to have a heart attack. She couldn't believe what I was saying. Ms. Brinks was silent, then she hung up in my face.

People expect principals to be perfect and show no emotion. They expect us to be the passive brunt of personal attacks without ever flinching or displaying human qualities. This is unrealistic and damn near impossible. Walking on water is not always possible but walking through it means that you stand on what's right. It's gonna get messy and you will come out of it tougher than you were when it all started. You stop worrying about appeasing people who are as wrong as two left feet. You get on with the business of leading and feel good about how you handled things because there's too much at stake to entertain foolishness for hours each day. You go home, kiss your wife and kids and have a wonderful evening. You rest well at night knowing that the decisions you make and the statements you make are grounded in what's fair and good for kids. You defend your people at all costs so that they know you've got their back. You take whatever heat comes down from the top because at the end of the day all of the calls come directly to you.

Chapter 16: The Year that Never Ended

Better is the end of a thing than its beginning, and the patient in spirit is better than the proud in spirit.
-Ecclesiastes 7:8

I WALKED THROUGH AN EMPTY SCHOOL IN EARLY APRIL OF 2020. I SAW THE COATS AND LITTLE JACKETS THEY LEFT AT SCHOOL ON THAT CHILLY MARCH AFTERNOON WHEN WE FIRST LEARNED THAT WE WOULD BE CLOSING OUR CAMPUS. "It'll only be for a few days", we all thought. I saw the lunches staff members left in the refrigerator in the staff lounge. I thought about how the hallways were once filled with energy and excitement each morning. Fourteen buses and hundreds of cars all bringing their scholars to spend the day with us. That was just a few weeks ago. The microphone in the cafeteria we once used to tell them to quiet down is still plugged in. Now, the silence is deafening. It's almost an apocalyptic scene of an urgent, unexpected departure from our familiar space. In the hallways there are displays of our class projects from February's Black History activities that are beginning to collapse onto the hallway floor. Posters around the school advertise school dances that went from being postponed to cancelled. In the classrooms, the dry erase boards are covered with the learning targets and activities with a date etched in time: March 12th. This was the last day that we saw our students and had a somewhat normal day of learning. At the time, we had no idea that we would not be together as a school for the remainder of the year.

We had so much left to celebrate this year. There were baby showers, teacher of the year announcements, retirements, and 5th graders to celebrate. We didn't realize that those moments would be taken away from us so suddenly. Now, we are left trying to find closure to a year that was snatched away from us all. When we do return, I think we will all appreciate one another a little more than we did before. I think we'll cherish what it means to be there for one another, not just to be there with one another. I think about the first-year teacher I hired and how this year will forever remain in her mind as a year that never truly ended. I think about the 3 student teachers from Georgia State University who were in the midst of their student teaching experience when all of this occurred. I wonder how they will move forward on their journey to become educators. I think about my scholars whose home lives were less than stable. I wonder how they will manage being 'sheltered in place' for months in their homes without the support of our staff members who were there for them.

The school felt like a museum today that was suddenly frozen in a moment, March 12th…awaiting our return. The vegetable garden is thriving, but the weeds are quickly gaining pace with the vegetables. The bells still ring at the times for arrival and dismissal. The phones are still ringing with calls from telemarketers. But no afternoon buses, no car rider dismissal, no mail delivery, no Fed Ex packages to sign for. It's an empty building awaiting the energy and the vibrancy that those 600 little people brought into the building each day. As much as we try to bring them instruction via virtual platforms, nothing replaces the feeling of having all of us together under one roof, learning, laughing, and experiencing what it means to be together as a school.

Now, we were all are trying to make sense of the new reality where we reach out to our scholars through virtual platforms each week. It was a drastic shift from our normal, but we were making it work as best as can be expected. With students in their homes for many weeks, parents and the community at large have a newfound appreciation for the role educators play in society. We nurture, we motivate, we comfort, and coach scholars to be better. We have those tough conversations with them and get them back on track. We were making progress and then it all came to a crashing halt. We started the year with professional goals and aspirations of what we'd accomplish together. We had no idea that we'd never get to finish all we started.

How do we move forward? We focus on being resilient. We accept the present reality for what it is. The future is uncertain, and we must accept that. With the announcement that the schools will remain closed in Georgia for the remainder of the year, we have to look forward. How do we foster the richest virtual learning communities we can in the coming weeks? While there's no replacement for the connectedness of a classroom filled with students and a dynamic teacher, we have to find a way to be in the present moment and navigate that space with love, compassion, and self-determination. Kendra Cherry writes about Self-determination theory, stating that people need three key things to get through psychologically tough times: Competence, connection and autonomy.

- "**Competence:** *People need to gain mastery of tasks and learn different skills. When people feel that they have the skills needed for success, they are more likely to take actions that will help them achieve their goals.*

- **Connection or Relatedness:** *People need to experience a sense of belonging and attachment to other people.*

- **Autonomy:** *People need to feel in control of their own behaviors and goals. This sense of being able to take direct action that will result in real change plays a major part in helping people feel self-determined.*"

We'll come out on the other side of this time with a renewed sense of purpose. We will be more connected, and we'll have new skills for delivering instruction in virtual platforms. But most important of all, we will feel a deeper sense of connection to those we've been separated from for months. I believe 2020, the school year that never ended, will also be the year that our vision becomes much clearer and we will finally be able to see the beauty and commonality we all possess. A year that never ended will afford us a chance at a very new and different beginning.

Working virtually has quickly gone from an option in the educational field to an absolute necessity under the Covid-19 global pandemic. Schools and universities are finding ways to reconnect people on platforms that help to keep the stream of collaboration and creativity flowing between educational professionals and the communities they serve. Colleges have sent students home to complete the semester online. Public schools have closed, and principals are bringing their teams together for conference calls and virtual meetings. I've never been a fan of bringing my team together out of compliance. If a meeting wasn't necessary, an email, pre-recorded virtual meeting or well-crafted document would suffice. High performing teams must have platforms to engage in productive collaboration that addresses challenges and allows the synergy of the collective genius of the organization to emerge in the midst of a crisis. Those in the trenches of this work of teaching virtually are not inclined to listen to long eloquent intellectual ramblings because time is of the essence. It's about time. So in this new landscape, it's important for those who lead to remember that honoring the time of your team is a wise and strategic leadership approach. Creating norms and structures around virtual teaming is critical to keep everyone engaged in the work.

Retreat for Strength

Each morning I retreat to my home office around 4am with a steaming cup of coffee and begin planning out the next several hours of priorities. In his book The 33 Strategies of War, Robert Greene writes, "Retreat in the face of a strong enemy is a sign not of weakness but of strength. By resisting the temptation to respond to an aggressor, you buy yourself valuable time – time to recover, to think, to gain perspective." In this case, our enemy is an invisible virus that has forced us all to retreat into our homes. At times though, the enemy can be our own weaknesses in the area of time management and productivity. Do you and members of your team have clearly defined methods of monitoring and managing your productivity

My Top 5

Last year, members of my team expressed how they were overwhelmed with emails about upcoming tasks and due dates. This led to me crafting a weekly list called *"My Top 5 Priorities for the Week"*. In one communication, they are able to quickly hone in on the top priorities for our school. It's about time. It was a time-related adjustment that I had to make as a school leader to better serve my team and the outcome was increased overall productivity. What adjustments are you making now as a leader to better meet the needs of your staff and students? We've quickly established new formats for ongoing professional learning for our staff that align to these new challenges. What can teachers begin learning right now to help them be more effective over the next 2-3 weeks? What evidence will they produce to show that they are now prepared to apply their learning to the work of the school? Adjustments are happening at all levels. Paraprofessionals are making calls after students view online lessons and providing support to students who need it. The time they spend working with students via phone or Facetime helps those students continue to stay engaged in academic content away from the school setting.

What is the point of this meeting?

The conference call is scheduled for 1:00. It's a busy Thursday afternoon in the midst of the second week of school closures. All 59 members of our teaching staff have been working remotely, frantically trying to keep our 600+ students engaged in meaningful tasks for the next several weeks. Like the rest of the nation's teaching force, it's a challenge that we were somewhat prepared for and have been executing well given the circumstances. We've pulled 15 members of our school leadership team together for this call, but the person facilitating the call doesn't seem to have direction or well-laid plan for the agenda. After team members respond, there are long pauses of silence. We are all waiting for the next point to be raised. Finally, someone chimes in, "Excuse me, I may have missed it, but what is the point of this meeting.". We all silently cheered that someone on the call had the nerve to say what we were all thinking. There was no meeting agenda shared prior to the meeting, and a clear purpose of the meeting had not been defined to honor the time of everyone on the call.

The 48-minute Mark

The Pomodoro Technique was developed in the late 1980's as a time management strategy to improve your overall productivity and creativity. It breaks down periods of work into shorter segments separated by breaks. For years, I've been using a variation of the Pomodoro Technique called the *48-minute rule*. It sets aside 48 minutes of uninterrupted work followed by 12 minutes of rest. Some have referred to it as the "Time Box Technique". For the last two weeks, my staff has held virtual staff meetings. The goal is to have a well-organized conference call that leaves everyone well informed of our priorities and with clear directives about next steps. There are two prerequisites I have for these meetings. First, there must be an agenda that is distributed to the team prior to the meeting. Secondly, at the outset of the meeting I provide a projected end time for the meeting. "Good afternoon everyone, thanks for joining us. We should be able to wrap things up in about 30-40 minutes. Let's get started." Eliminating the uncertainty of purpose helps our team to remain focused on the agenda. If a meeting is reaching the 48 minute mark, members of my team know that I'm likely going to begin to wrap things up by saying, "We are approaching the 48-minute mark…" as a suggestion to determine if we need to push forward or whether we need to pause and reconvene at a later time once we've digested the information. I'm always open to continue as long as the discussion is purposeful and productive.

So now, droves of teachers and students around the country are at home, managing their own time. Far removed from the bells, class changes, and dismissal structures that provided structure to the normal school day. Leaders and teachers should make it a priority to share virtual schedules with families to help them structure the time away from the classroom. There are still due dates, high priority tasks and assignments to be completed daily, but the challenge now is creating a structure that leads to getting things done. Likewise, teachers are charged with being even more structured in designing their day with clear objectives and priorities listed on a daily schedule. Many members of my team are juggling the responsibilities of caring for their own children, helping them with their schoolwork, and also teaching virtually. They are learning new platforms, updating websites, assessing student work and being attentive husbands and wives. In the familiar confines of our homes the temptation is much greater to get distracted by technology and other household tasks. The number one task of an educational leader in the crosshairs of the Covid-19 pandemic is to (1) be sensitive to the emotional stress of the pandemic culture and how it is affecting everyone, and to (2) effectively manage my time and to honor the time of those with whom I work and serve. Our communities need us. The beautiful irony of it all is that in the separation, we are given the opportunity to unite. In our retreat, we are given the opportunity to advance. There is no perfect planner or journal that will be the key to our productivity and success. It ultimately boils down to how we manage every minute and hour of the day. At the end of the day, it's about time.

Chapter 17: Guarding the Gates

"For a wide door for effective work has opened to me, and there are many adversaries.
1 Corinthians 16:9

A FTER YEARS OF ANTICIPATION, THE ORACLE OF EAST ORANGE HAD FINALLY SPOKEN. MS. LAURYN HILL TAPPED INTO THAT TIMELESS SPACE WHERE *"HIP-HOP MEETS SCRIPTURE"* WITH THE APTLY TITLED "GUARDING THE GATES" FROM THE QUEEN AND SLIM SOUNDTRACK. The opening lines convey the litany of questions posed to those who are perpetually seeking greater. The song's title suggests that there are things of great value just beyond the gates, hence the need for them to be guarded. Shortly after I accepted my first assistant principalship in Washington State, I was in a 4th floor office looking out over the city of Tacoma having a conversation with the deputy superintendent. He asked me, "So, you are coming here from Georgia. The question is, are you running from something or running to something?" As I listened to Lauryn's words, she brought me back to this conversation and about how movement evokes questions.

Guarding the Gates is an anthem of self-discovery and self-preservation. In another sense, it can be included in the playlist of those of us looking to guard the gates of our professions from those entering with the wrong intentions, bias, and misperceptions about the purpose of our work. In 2013, I was invited to speak with a gymnasium filled with new teachers in the Richmond County School System. The title of my talk was "The Flight to Success". I didn't want to read a speech with dry quotes sprinkled with educational jargon. I wanted to find a way to connect the anxiety of entering the profession with the feelings that we have as we embark on a flight. I compared their arrival into this profession with arriving at the Hartsfield-Jackson International Airport in Atlanta filled with travelers scrambling to get to different destinations. Upon arrival at the counter, they'd be asked these questions:

- May I see your ID?
- What's your destination?
- Do you have any baggage you'd like to check?
- Has anyone placed anything in your bags without your knowledge?

Each of the questions speaks to knowing who you are, where you are going, checking unnecessary baggage, and guarding your gates from negativity or destructive thinking. It was an analogy that connected well with the audience. They laughed as I gave examples of travelers carrying excessive baggage and incurring additional charges. It was a light-hearted story, but there was a layer of truth beneath the humor. A fear of flying can keep many travelers from their destinations. They become obsessed with all that could possibly go wrong. What if the plane crashes or runs out of fuel? A fear of flying can keep you from making a departure at the right time. Knowing when to leave an organization is another form of guarding the gates. If the direction of the district, non-profit, or corporation is moving steadily away from your core values, stepping away is always the best option to stay true to who you are and where you are planning to go.

Approaching the Gates: Vulnerability

Long before gaining access to the boarding gates, all travelers are subjected to a screening. You are asked to remove items from your pockets. You are reminded to remove your shoes. Your bags are thoroughly scanned. Some of the unluckiest of us are even subjected to a search by TSA agents. Vulnerability and leadership go hand in hand. Courageous leaders find the right moments to be vulnerable and pull back the veil of their own areas of growth. In the Forbes article *Could a Little Vulnerability Be the Key to Better Leadership*, Carley Sime writes, "Vulnerable leaders are ideally motivated to use and share their vulnerability to develop and grow into better leaders, to model the power of vulnerability and courage and create an environment where the workforce is able to do the same. Overarching this is hopefully a desire to progress and develop the organization and workforce."

Guarding the gates means sensing when the tides are changing and determining next steps. Leaders of organizations have to be careful to not lose their best employees by building restrictive gates around the innovation and autonomy of creatives. Lauryn Hill, with her arrivals into and departures from the public eye on her own schedule, is the embodiment of artistic freedom. Her movements remind us of our own responsibility to guard ourselves from becoming pawns of organizations, school districts, or companies whose priorities are aligned to their strategic plans and not in tune with our own eclectic rhythms and syncopation. Rather than becoming preoccupied with others' interpretations of her movements, she writes:

> "What you say to me, I don't mind at all, What you say to me, I don't really care at all, 'Cause I'm in love, Tryna fix myself for society, Trying to mix myself for society, But can you tell me where is love in anxiety"

Metaphoric Gates

The metaphor of gates as barriers to movement can be found in other songs. Whether on the inside of the gates in our safe spaces, or outside the gates hoping to break through the barriers obstructing our path, we have to make decisions and maintain momentum. Guarding the gates means staying true to who I am as a writer, educator, entrepreneur, and school leader. It means never allowing those aspects of my personality to be locked outside of my work. In the second verse of Goodie Mob's *Cell Therapy*, the creatively *uncaged* Cee-Lo Green ends his verse questioning the real purpose of the gates in his housing project: "But every now and then, I wonder if the gate was put up to keep crime out or keep our ass in."

Chapter 18: The Courage to Fight

T HERE ARE MANY MOMENTS WHEN I TAKE TIME TO
TALK WITH STUDENTS ABOUT HOW TO DISPLAY
COURAGE. In order for our young people to
understand how to embody courage, we must
show them examples of those who have
confronted obstacles and risked comfort for the
sake of progress. Individuals who put the needs
of the group before their own are the example of courage our
young people need to see. Muhammad Ali is a perfect example
of this. Between 1967 and 1970 he was banned from boxing for
refusing to participate in the Vietnam War. He lost his title, was
sentenced to five years in prison, and fined $10,000 as a result of
his decision. A contemporary example of this is Colin Kaepernick,
whom I mention in my book, *The Mountain Principles: Lessons on
Leading & Learning.* Both Ali and Kaepernick engaged in noble
fights on behalf of others.

People driven by a cause and purpose are relentless. They
are undeterred when it comes to moving around or through

obstacles. Along with the other 115,000 other school principals around the nation, I'm fighting for the quality of the education of our children. The fight is ideological, philosophical, and theoretical. The opponents in the fight vary depending on the circumstances. At any given moment, the opposing parties could be publishers, vendors, politicians, parents, or media outlets. Regardless of the opponent, the fight ensues daily.

Rather than going through the motions, I want to unravel the tangled pieces of public schooling, with the help of a talented team of educators, and create spaces where students thrive and grow in ways that aren't necessarily measured by normed referenced tests. How do we get beyond where we are now as a school and community and push forward? **It is a noble fight.**

Another fight worth fighting is for the autonomy of teachers to be creative and innovative in their practices. We've traveled light years beyond the days when my teachers stood in front of the class holding a teacher's edition reading off pre-printed directions to the class. Teachers have the world at their fingertips and can extend the classroom to other states, countries, and galaxies using instructional technology. The unfettered genius of teachers should never be stifled. Teachers are professionals and should be treated as such. As long as the curriculum is being taught, I love to see teachers integrating students' interests, the arts, and discussion into the curriculum. Standardization is a mixed bag of guidance, clarity, and constraints on creativity that can dull the luster of a brilliant educator if thrust upon them irresponsibly. The fight is to find the delicate balance between teaching standards and teaching the child in a way that meets their needs. **It is a worthy fight.**

The fight for the respect of the profession is one that principals should be prepared to join. Respect their time. Respect their intellect. Respect their voice. For the most part, parents understand that teachers are professionals and treat them as such. However, there is a small subset of parents who engage teachers and schools in a verbally aggressive manner unbefitting of the role that teachers play in our children's lives. Profanity laced text messages, veiled threats, and unreasonable demands are poor models of interaction for our students. When parents engage in these behaviors, leaders should gracefully step in to support teachers in a way that teaches the appropriate behavior and establishes clear norms for how teachers will be treated. Teachers prepare for this work by completing years of education, certification tests, graduate school, and a wealth of ongoing professional development. They deserve the respect that is afforded to any professional. Sometimes that respect is shown by simply bringing a valid concern to the teacher before escalating it to the administration. The fight for the respect of the profession is real. **It is a righteous fight.**

Edgar Albert Guest describes the drive to fight a righteous fight in the most eloquent way in his poem titled "Courage":

Courage isn't a brilliant dash,
A daring deed in a moment's flash;
It isn't an instantaneous thing
Born of despair with a sudden spring
It isn't a creature of flickered hope
Or the final tug at a slipping rope;
But it's something deep in the soul of man
That is working always to serve some plan.
Courage isn't the last resort
In the work of life or the game of sport;
It isn't a thing that a man can call
At some future time when he's apt to fall;
If he hasn't it now, he will have it not
When the strain is great and the pace is hot.
For who would strive for a distant goal
Must always have courage within his soul.
Courage isn't a dazzling light
That flashes and passes away from sight;
It's a slow, unwavering, ingrained trait
With the patience to work and the strength to wait.
It's part of a man when his skies are blue,
It's part of him when he has work to do.
The brave man never is freed of it.
He has it when there is no need of it.
Courage was never designed for show;
It isn't a thing that can come and go;
It's written in victory and defeat
And every trial a man may meet.
It's part of his hours, his days and his years,
Back of his smiles and behind his tears.
Courage is more than a daring deed:
It's the breath of life and a strong man's creed.

Edgar Albert Guest

Chapter 19: Doorways

THERE IS MUCH SYMBOLISM AROUND THE IDEA OF A DOOR. DOORWAYS REPRESENT TRANSITIONS FROM ONE PLACE TO ANOTHER. THE DOORWAY IS WHERE OUR GUESTS ARE WELCOMED INTO A HOME OR A SCHOOL. The doorway is where first impressions are made. Our language is sprinkled with idioms alluding to the significance of doors:

- When one door closes, another one opens
- Showing somebody the door
- To get one's foot in the door

As we celebrate graduations and students begin to walk out of our school doors and prepare to enter other doors in the fall, it is important to let them acknowledge the mix of emotions that come along with those changes. When students leave elementary school, it's a bittersweet moment for many of them. While they have excitement about what awaits them in middle school, many are equally nervous about being the new students on campus. That feeling of anxiousness is absolutely normal and will gradually turn to excitement as the first day of middle school draws closer.

As I speak to my students and their families at luncheons and evening events, I sometimes recount an experience I had that helped me learn 5 valuable lessons for life. Unlike most of my classmates, my Saturday mornings were typically spent going from door to door teaching from the Bible and sharing and discussing religious publications. After a hard knock on the door there were those moments of uncertainty. Will they answer? Who will answer? How will they respond?

Here's what that experience taught me:

Persistence: Sometimes in life you will have to knock more than once before a door will open. Whether it's a job you interview for, a scholarship you pursue, or a team you try out for, you have to be able to bounce back if things don't happen the first time. Be persistent, patient, and attentive.

Preparation: Once the door opens, be ready. Know what you will say and deliver it like you believe it. Review your notes. Practice in the mirror. First impressions are powerful, so make sure that you make the best of those first few seconds when the door of opportunity opens.

Probability: The odds are that some doors will not open for you. Every opportunity you pursue in life will not be successful. Accept that and move forward.

Persona: The moment of truth was the moment when a classmate opened the door. I learned that your best self at the door had to be parallel to your best self at the school. Avoid the confusion of having to play different characters in different contexts. Be you all the time.

Poise: Be self-confident and willing to receive new information. Understand that sometimes the person the other side of the door may possess a perspective or information to take you further or deeper than you ever imagined. Be aware that at times people will say harsh things to elicit a response. Take the high road.

Go out there and walk up those steps. Your best life is waiting on the other side of the door. Knock hard.

When I think of visionary educators, the folks who opened the doors for me in this profession, I think of Lucy Craft Laney and Marva Collins. Both women started their own schools in predominately African-American communities. Laney opened the doors of her school in 1883 in Augusta, Georgia while Collins would open the doors of Westside Preparatory School during the same year I was born – 1975. A solid elementary foundation was at the core of both their philosophies. In 2012, I had the opportunity to visit the famed Ron Clark Academy in Atlanta, GA. In many ways, Ron Clark Academy stands on the shoulders Marva Collins' Westside Preparatory School National Training Institute which provided teachers with opportunities to visit and gain professional development as they saw the principles in action in a real setting with real students. Laney and Collins were able to leave remarkable legacies as educators without large corporate sponsorships, federal funding or dance routines.

Marva Collins' story in particular, is one of grit and sheer resolve to instill a desire to learn in students. Her school, once located in Chicago's Southside, operated free of federal funds. This kept it free of many of restrictions and mandates that accompany those monies. From a purely administrative standpoint, this approach to instructional autonomy alone made Westside Preparatory School a brilliant approach to the education of young scholars. Most administrators, including myself, depend upon Title I funds and spend a considerable amount of time trying to remain in compliance and meet the needs of our students and families.

My academic and intellectual relationship with Marva Collins and her school is a circuitous one. I met her personally as a second-year teacher in Macon, Georgia. In 2002, weary from a long day of teaching, we were summoned to an unusually warm office complex that the district used for professional development. A mix of excitement and fatigue loomed in the air of the large room that appeared to be designed for a considerably smaller crowd. For the next two hours, we were all swept away into a Shakespearean stream of high expectations, tight routines, and relentless questioning and prompting. Her comments were direct, her humor and wit were precise, and her charge to us was to be uncompromising because the lives of children were at stake. *"I don't wear a name tag"* she said. *"Never did! It's my job to tell you who I am. That's what we have to teach children. Speak up for yourself. Make your presence known."* Her concepts were so simple, yet they pushed squarely against the prevailing notions of the teaching act.

Later that evening, I went online and read everything I could find about Marva Collins, including the 60 Minutes segment that featured her students reflecting on their experience at Westside Preparatory School.

Fifteen years after that meeting, I became the principal of a school founded on the concepts of Westside Preparatory School. The school is grounded in a culture of high expectations and supported by parents who agree to dedicate 16 hours of time to the school each year. Students memorize poetry, complete semester projects, morning meetings are conducted, and uniforms are worn. But those are tertiary requirements. What's critical for converging with Marva Collins' philosophy is establishing a pervasive culture of high academic expectations where students are challenged to step out of their comfort zones, speak in front of their peers, and write about their experiences.

I first found myself grappling with Marva Collins ideologically when I began reading "Ordinary Students, Extraordinary Teachers". Getting past the title took a moment. I don't see any "ordinary students" because I see how extraordinary so many of our students are given their talent, drive, and complex circumstances. Beyond the cover page, the book is a beautiful collection of her writings that inspire and challenge my thinking in the same ways that she did in Macon in 2002. While we disagree on the emphasis on whole group reading instruction and her suggestion that the small reading groups should be disbanded, we find common ground on her approach to phonics and teaching the many ways one sound is made so that students see all the spellings at once (i.e. ck, k, c) as opposed to introducing them separately.

In "Marva Collins' Way", she delves into her approach on teaching Macbeth and other Shakespearean writings to five-year olds. As I read it I'm inspired and interested in how to integrate the classics into the elementary curriculum in a more rigidly structured, high-stakes testing educational setting. It is at this point that our approaches diverge once more. My students, mostly African-American, African, and Hispanic, thirst for images and stories that connect to their experiences and their culture. Culturally responsive classrooms and schools lay a psychological foundation for students that starts with them becoming more culturally and personally aware of who they are. This prepares them to develop an appreciation for others' cultures, languages, and perspectives.

This idea of grappling with an author is something that I learned studying with Dr. Daniel Chapman in Georgia Southern University's Curriculum Studies program. Too often, we pull from the text without fully challenging the assertions of the author, examining the context, and demanding more justification for a perspective. As educators, we comb through articles and books looking for ideas we can implement in our schools. Reading and thinking critically about issues insulates us in a culture that often seeks simple solutions to complex problems. As we stumble upon gems, we inevitably must toss aside portions of the readings that either don't align with what we believe or reflects time and context, funding-wise or testing-wise, vastly different from our reality.

Arguments with Mrs. Collins help me find my footing as a leader. I'm not willing to allow a few divergent perspectives to negate the immense wisdom found in her writings. That would be foolish. So as I argue and wrestle with her ideologically, I'm growing in my instructional prowess and reminded that while we may not agree on every issue, we are working for the same cause: educating children well.

Each year, one of the most exciting events in our Field Day festivities is the Tug of War. This classic game, which originated in ancient ceremonies in many cultures, involves teams pulling together to pull the opposing team in their direction. At our school, the tug of war is a matter of pride among classes. Teams wear colors to show support for one another and team coaches make sure that participants are positioned in key spots along the rope.

There are some keys to winning the game though.

1. *Dig your feet into the ground when you start to pull.*
2. *Always work together as a team because no one person can win.*
3. *Take small steps.*
4. *Participants of various strengths should be in different positions.*

In the Fall of 2019, we held our first PTA meeting of the year. As the crowd began to fill up the chairs in our cafeteria, we quickly realized that we were running out of seats. After 450 seats were in place, we still had nearly 40 people standing. These are the dilemmas you want to have in a school. PTA is a cornerstone of a successful school community. It is the voice, engine and fundraising arm of much of what goes on at a school. It also offers a platform to clarify misconceptions or explain policies to ensure everyone on the team is not just holding the rope, but also pulling in the right direction.

I wanted to illustrate this with our actual tug of war rope from PE. I brought it out and asked one of my PTA officers to come hold the rope. She immediately held it from an opposing stance. She was positioned to pull against the principal. Voila! It was a perfect illustration of how we are prepared to be in opposition to that very entity we should be pulling with. I asked her to reposition herself so that we are pulling in the same direction because nothing really happens when we are pulling against one another. It was a tangible and visible illustration of how to change how we advocate for our children.

The problem is **not** that we lack people willing to pull. The problem is we aren't always pulling in the same direction. Repositioning our efforts and aligning our power is the key to getting things accomplished. The school community five types of tuggers:

- The Pullers - they pull in the right direction as hard as they can.
- **The Play Callers**: they tell others to pull harder while watching from the side.

- **The Opposers**: they pull against the very team they are on.
- **The Rope Managers**: they pull and reposition people in the right place, so victory is certain.
- **The Potential Pullers** - they place their hands on the rope (show up), but never really pull.

As I sat on the stage and looked out at the standing room only crowd, I realized that we have enough people pulling in the same direction to overpower those who are pulling against our success. But that's not the ultimate goal. The goal is to have them repositioned to pull alongside us. We need them. We've been working on developing that critical mass of supporters to help us implement change and support new initiatives. Tonight was confirmation that we are successful in our efforts. I recently read the article "Sustaining Change by Achieving a Critical Mass" by Siobhan Brown. Brown writes that during the implementation phase "the old and the new systems are competing for survival. People will feel a range of emotions from anger, resentment, and resignation to relief and excitement."

Each year our team plans six events to provide parents with an hour to have access to the principal to address any concerns, pose question or offer suggestions. The sessions, billed as "Meet with Mr. Mountain", are my way of carving out time to help ensure we are, in fact, pulling in the same direction. Implementing change starts with the other leaders in the building. Empowering them with the facts and the rationale behind changes and policies has ripple effects in influencing those pulling for our success. We can't lose if we are all pulling in the same direction.

Epilogue: Canaries in the Mine

Futures made of virtual insanity now
Always seem to, be governed by this love we have
For useless, twisting, our new technology
Oh, now there is no sound for we all live underground
And I'm thinking what a mess we're in
Hard to know where to begin
If I could slip the sickly ties that earthly man has made

-Jamiroquai, Virtual Insanity

AN INFLUENZA PANDEMIC SPREADS ACROSS THE NATION IN 1918 AND 1919. AS THE CASES GROW, OFFICIALS ACROSS THE COUNTRY DECIDE TO CLOSE SCHOOLS. New York and Chicago decide to keep their schools open and send health care workers into the schools to closely monitor the conditions of the students and hygiene practices. In nine cities across the nation, inter-agency conflict erupts. The Board of Health in Baltimore orders schools to be reopened. The Board of Education defies the order and closes the schools indefinitely in the midst of the pandemic. In some communities, Italian immigrants are blamed for spreading the virus. The nation was in turmoil and the agencies tasked with unraveling the conundrum were at odds with one another as the plight of the nation and its children hung the balance.

A crowd gathers outside a school board meeting in Augusta on a unusually warm July afternoon in 2020 to protest the cancellation of graduations. The temperatures and the months of restrictions are beginning to heighten the tension. The crowd consists of people of all ethnicities and ages ranging from disappointed high school students to concerned parents. The district's board of education is inside conducting a virtual meeting while just outside the doors a group assembles, some masked, some unmasked, to express their frustration with the decision to cancel graduations. It's a scene that is playing out in cities across the country. The city's mayor has issued a mask mandate, but the governor has countered that it can't be enforced. Two hundred miles west in Atlanta, a similar conflict is playing out between the same governor and Mayor Bottoms. While the governor has not mandated masks be worn by the general public, but the mayor has issued a mandate that masks be worn given the spike in Covid-19 cases and CDC projections.

It is virtual insanity as agencies and policies collide. Parents find themselves caught in the crosshairs of what's best for their children and what's feasible for their work schedules. Some explore homeschool options, others are in desperate need of schools to reopen so that they can resume work in coming weeks. When polled, the responses from parents are equally split between a return to traditional classes, a hybrid model of instruction, and virtual instruction for the start of the school year.

Five months into the global pandemic, the 45th occupant of the White House threatens to withhold funding to schools unless they reopen. The Secretary of Education contradicts the recommendations of the CDC and makes a press run downplaying the risk of reopening schools. Meanwhile the CDC reports that there have been over three million cases of Covid-19 and over 135,000 confirmed deaths as a result of Covid-19. These astonishing numbers are continuing to rise even as schools remain closed since mid-March.

The push to reopen schools without ongoing discussions inclusive of the professionals directly impacted by these decisions negates the protections needed for our teachers, administrators and most importantly our children. The reduction in school nurses in schools such as the one I lead has put our schools at a strategic disadvantage in monitoring and responding to the healthcare needs of children at school. This is not another task we can add to the plates of teachers. Some have talked about having teachers take the temperatures of students as they enter classrooms. Details are still inconsistent on what a traditional classroom would look like under the recommendations provided by the CDC.

Canaries in the Mine

We can't rush back to a normal existence because normal no longer exists. The National Center for Education Statistics notes that 20% of U.S. teachers are 55 years or older. Many of the educators that fall into this group suffer from underlying health conditions, putting them at greater risk of infection. The principal's first task is to ensure the safety of the student and staff under our leadership. Keeping them safe means keeping them apart for now and launching into virtual learning to start the school year. It's the best course of action until we see significant decreases in cases and mortality nationwide. We must not allow our students to be used at the litmus test for herd immunity from Covid-19. What the administration is suggesting is reminiscent of the use of canaries in British coal mines, a practice that started as early as 1911. Miners would take canaries into the mines because if there were carbon monoxide present or other poisonous gases, the canaries would be affected first, signaling to the miners that they needed to exit the mine. This moment requires leaders willing to take a stand on behalf of our most vulnerable. Our children and schools can't be intimidated and coerced into placing educators and families in harm's way as the federal government tries to figure it out. The interagency conflict of the early 1900's has revisited us. Health officials are under fire for making points of clarification on news outlets in an effort to better inform the public.

Instead, we will create virtual spaces to reach our students, and when the appropriate time comes, we will continue moving public education into a space where other nations and American higher education has been for decades – a fully-equipped hybrid educational model for P-12. Research has proven that all students learn differently. Every child does not need to walk into a school building each day to receive a high-quality education. There are some students who need that structure and socialization each day, but there are groups of students who would thrive much better in a different type of structure that we will now be able to provide as an option moving forward. For far too long we've lagged behind the private sector in the way we use technology in public education. Let's revamp the profession from the inside out starting with teacher preparation in colleges, professional development in districts, and ongoing professional learning for leaders.

I miss all of my students, but I'm especially disappointed in not being able to welcome our newest Pre-K and Kindergarten students. I imagine a five-year old who is looking forward to the first day of Pre-K or Kindergarten, but sadly won't have the experience of holding mom and dad's hand as they walk to the classroom for the first time. They won't get to sit on the carpet this fall and talk about their summer. The playgrounds will remain empty for a time. But in this expansive chess match of politics and policy, they will be safer at home as young kings and queens in quarantine and not pawns in peril. We will not allow them to be canaries in a mine.

Index

Notes:

Notes:

Photo by Ryan Manning

About the Author

André Benito Mountain is an author and educator who resides in metro-Atlanta with his family. He has written articles for national and international education publications. His previous books include *The Brilliance Beneath* and *The Mountain Principles*. He and his daughter are the founders of Def-ED Clothing. Mr. Mountain received a BA in History from Georgia Southern University and an MA in Elementary Education from Wesleyan College. He also holds an Ed.S. in Educational Administration from Augusta University.

Contact André Benito Mountain:

Email: DefEducation@icloud.com

www.andrebenitomountain.com

Other books by André Benito Mountain:

The Brilliance Beneath: The Power of Perspective in Urban Schools
ISBN-13: 978-1530639939

The Mountain Principles: Lessons on Leading and Learning
ISBN-13: 978-1726811170

Made in the USA
Monee, IL
29 January 2021